C000163217

Acknowledgements

Cover designs by Neil Parkes, Copperhead Studios,
copperheadstudios@hotmail.com

Front cover photo of the Radcliffe Camera in the snow by
Birte Milne

Rear cover photo of Magdalen Woods, Oxford by Neil Parkes

All profits will be shared with
Maggie's Cancer Information Centre, Oxford
www.maggiescentres.org

Also by The Turl Street Writers:

Being John Black
Turl Street Tales

Midwinter Tales

The Turl Street Writers

Published 2010 by arima publishing

www.arimapublishing.com

ISBN 978 1 84549 426 1

© Contributors 2010
All rights reserved

This book is copyright. Subject to statutory exception and to provisions of relevant collective licensing agreements, no part of this publication may be reproduced, stored in a retrieval system, or transmitted in any form or by any means, without the prior written permission of the authors.

Printed and bound in the United Kingdom

Typeset in Garamond 12/14

This book is sold subject to the conditions that it shall not, by way of trade or otherwise, be lent, re-sold, hired out, or otherwise circulated without the publisher's prior consent in any form of binding or cover other than that which it is published and without a similar condition including this condition being imposed on the subsequent purchaser.

In this work of fiction, the characters, places and events are either the product of the authors' imagination or they are used entirely fictitiously. The moral rights of the authors have been asserted. Any resemblance to actual persons, living or dead, is purely coincidental.

Swirl is an imprint of arima publishing.

arima publishing
ASK House, Northgate Avenue
Bury St Edmunds, Suffolk IP32 6BB
t: (+44) 01284 700321
www.arimapublishing.com

Contents

Melting Moment
Neil Hancox

The snow lay round about deep and crisp and even, and Motherwife was frazzled. The children were importuning her, begging to investigate the parcels stacked under the tree and husband was wallowing in a warm bed complaining of a hangover from last night's festivities. In the kitchen the great unwashed – carrots, sprouts and potatoes – and the great unstuffed – turkey – awaited her ministrations.

"Get up, salute the happy morn," she sang as she flicked the duvet away from her slumbering man, exposing purple pyjamas and white flesh. With ill-concealed grace he tumbled to the floor and assumed his winter woollies. Foredressed was forewarmed.

The family assembled round the breakfast table. Jimmy and his younger sister Cecilia were buzzing with excitement while Father was pleading for quiet. They expected a greeting of 'Happy Christmas.' Instead they were welcomed with plates of steaming porridge. Three stomachs rebelled, anticipating better things later in the day, but in the end hunger won and lumps of goodness crashed down the gullet onto the remains of last night's supper. Groans, grunts and belches rent the air as the stressed Motherwife apportioned tasks to keep her brood from beneath her feet while she decorated, diced, decocted and cooked.

Duly discharged, man and children retired to the lounge. There was no newspaper on Christmas Day and the battered old TV set was being temperamental. Christmas presents represented temptation which must be resisted until after dinner.

Cecilia, a very imaginative seven-year-old, had convinced her brother that Motherwife had a shotgun in the umbrella stand and would use it on the first person to interfere with wrapping paper and ribbon before the appointed time. To clinch the matter she reminded her brother that Motherwife had recently taken up woodwork. She said that she was making a bookcase but it did look very like a coffin. Grown-ups did not always tell the truth. Father took a more prosaic view. Nevertheless with Motherwife in frazzle mode it paid to be cautious.

Jimmy looked at Cecilia. Cecilia looked at Father. Father looked at Jimmy. They all looked at the snow, until, with one voice, they exclaimed, "Let's build a snowman."

Wellies joined woollies, gloves covered hands, and hats covered ears, as the three adventurers poured forth into the garden screaming and shouting. Snowballs flew, followed by curses, suitably muted, as Father was repeatedly hit. As his assailants paused for breath he assumed senior project manager mode.

"You," he shouted at Jimmy, "start shovelling. Cecilia, you start rolling the snow up into a concentric structure."

"What's concentric?" Cecilia begged of her older brother. He didn't know, but using a smidgeon of common sense (something rare in this family) made a guess, a good guess, and soon an obese, five-foot high structure arose like a wraith. The children were dispatched to fetch hat, scarf, pipe and sundry vegetables, with which to render the simulacrum more lifelike.

The scarf, from a venerable Oxford college, was wrapped around the neck of the figure. Onions and shallots made the buttons and a nose, and a carrot served in the pursuit of manly verisimilitude. As no pipe was forthcoming, a lighted *Gauloise* was slipped between the frozen lips, giving a certain European air to the creation. A glass of steaming grog, from which Father surreptitiously supped, was placed within reach of the right hand and Grandad's bowler used to complete the tableau.

Cecilia paused to admire their work and as she did so, she thought that she saw a tear roll down a smooth, white cheek. She shivered. Snowmen don't cry. Was something missing? A heart, of course. She fetched a red pepper from the kitchen, pushed it into the centre of the frozen chest and was rewarded with a smile.

The snowman was named Mr Black by a politically aware Jimmy and photographed from all angles, though as Father explained, because of the excess of reflected light, all the photographs would be washed out. In reality he had forgotten how to work this damned digital device.

Motherwife, transformed into snow queen in a glistening gown, sapphire tiara and white sable boots, and thoroughly de-frazzled by the absence of her dearly beloveds and possibly a liberal helping of cooking sherry, came out, inspected and started to approve. As she did so she felt the sadness of her family's creation and saw an ephemeral creature seeking love. She kept her thoughts to herself and bade her family to table.

Once seated they swapped woolly hats for paper ones and traded excruciating jokes from the great Chinese joke emporium, as Father thrust a two-pronged fork into a bronzed breast releasing odours and juices to quicken their jaded appetites. Jimmy and Cecilia toasted one another in lemonade while Motherwife and Father raised glasses of champagne. Flaming plum pudding and custard followed and both Jimmy and Cecilia, by dint of careful parental administrations, avoided swallowing hidden antique half-crowns.

The nuclear family, re-fused in harmony, lay round about the glowing hearth, deep and crisp and even.

As the children were released upon their presents, and Father dozed, the snow queen slipped away and led her snowman off to softer shores where her melting warmth would eventually reveal a red pepper.

Getting Away for Christmas
Graham Bird

Albert yawned and turned over, the condensation from his breath floating away as he pulled the starched sheets to his chin. He squinted at the morning sun that spilled through the lace curtains, and then he sat bolt upright, wide awake and looked around.

The room was dirty white and his narrow bed was squeezed up against the wall, leaving just enough room for a single wardrobe and table. A washbowl sat on the table next to a large white jug. The room smelled of tobacco; Albert didn't smoke, not since his father had died. He walked over to the window, wrapping a blanket around his naked body, and scraped his finger down the ice-covered glass. He could just see the source of a noise, the clipping of horseshoes on the cobbles outside as a hackney carriage passed. The cabman and horse were the only living beings he could see, alone together in an icy bright world of unfamiliar buildings and streets. The air was still and somewhere, very far away, he could hear church bells.

There was a knock at the door but before Albert could speak, it opened. He pulled the blanket closer. A young woman entered with a tray of steaming tea.

"Oh, sorry sir, I do beg your pardon. I thought you'd still be asleep."

"I can't sleep at all. Not sure I have. What time is it?"

"Seven o'clock, sir. I've brought you some tea and toast. You need to eat, sir, and you must be freezing. I'll fetch you some hot water and we'll get you downstairs to the fireside when you're ready."

Albert watched the girl pour tea into a large china cup. He noticed a small crack all down one side, not that he had any thought to complain. "What's your name?" he said.

"Milly, sir."

"Call me Albert, please. I'm not one to be staying in inns usually, really I'm not."

"I'll try sir... Albert." Milly smiled at him, and Albert's whole body felt warmer.

"Where are all the others?" he said.

"Oh, many of them are here. I've heard that some are in the Randolph, but that's probably those with money. Here at the King's Arms, we're just trying to help out as much as we can. All the rooms are full. Me and the girls have come in specially to help. I was going to be off today."

Albert gazed at the young woman as she chatted, and sipped slowly at the tea.

"I'll get dressed and come down," he said.

"Yes, of course, sir... Albert. I'll fetch you that hot water. By the way, I know this is difficult, but, well... Happy Christmas."

As Milly closed the door, he sat back on the bed, resting his head against the wall and thought about George.

*

Albert pushed through the crowds, clutching his brown leather case to his chest. Everything he owned was in there, his change of clothes, his shaving brush and razor, and a small notebook tied with string containing some postcards and a photo of his mother and sister.

The queue at the ticket booth stretched all along the back wall of platform 1 where there was a line of coffee stalls and food sellers. Albert took in the aromas of baking bread mixed with the sooty steam from the locomotives, sighing and hissing their displeasure at the icy wind and flurries of snow. It seemed that everyone was going somewhere else, probably to reunite with their families for the seasonal celebrations but Albert suspected at least a few were escaping like him, the wonder of the modern railway splitting up families and friends.

He had never been on a train. He'd seen them of course, trundling over the bridge next to his sister's shabby flat, where he'd left the note earlier that morning. He had visited Paddington soon after it opened, just to stand in awe at the number of engines, coaches and people in one place with all that steel and glass. Albert had only been out of London once, visiting an uncle in St Albans. Thirty-five years in the slums of St Giles and he knew it was time to go.

"Second class single to Wolverhampton please, my boy."

Albert watched as the man in front put down a new pound note on the table. He was wearing a grey suit with freshly cleaned black shoes, and carried a small black bag. A porter stood next to him with a trolley of luggage, all neatly labelled 'Mr G Smith, Edgware'.

Well, I guess that's as good a place as any, thought Albert, not that he'd ever heard of Wolverhampton. Albert had not thought about where he'd go until that moment. He knew he had to run, to get away from scraping a living for the last twenty-eight years, always on the edge of the law, always one step ahead.

Once, he'd worked as a porter at the Seven Dials Inn and that was his best job until he was caught thieving from a gentleman. Then he worked in a bakery and each day he managed to steal enough to set up a small street stall serving tea, bread and butter to the gentry in the evening on their way to the Theatre Royal. One evening, the master baker walked by and that ended that. All of Albert's schemes came to nothing eventually.

His sister rescued him every time, letting him sleep on her floor and giving him food. But this time, he repaid her by stealing ten shillings from her purse and he knew he'd gone too far, especially when her boyfriend caught him red-handed.

'Happy Christmas my Janey, you'll be better without me for a while. I'll be in touch. Sorry about the money, love Alby.'

"Second class single to Wolverhampton, please," said Albert.

"Four shillings, sir. Platform 3 at ten o'clock. It might be a bit late with this frosty start today, and with such a crowd on Christmas Eve."

Albert hurried to follow his Mr Smith as they jostled their way across the station and along the platform toward the front carriage.

He boarded just behind the porter, helping him with Mr Smith's largest case, then put his own bag on the rack and settled in the window seat.

"Freezing cold as usual. These damn trains never get any better," said Mr Smith.

"It's my first time. Trip to Wolverhampton for Christmas," smiled Albert.

The ten o'clock pulled out a few minutes late, and sliced its way slowly through the white Berkshire blanket of snow. The two men chatted amiably and found they had much in common. Albert was good at having things in common with people.

"Visiting relatives?" George asked.

"I'm staying with my aunt for Christmas," Albert lied. "And you?"

"Well, actually, no. As it happens my aunt died last month, and I'm going up to sort out her affairs. She was my only relative. I didn't know her at all, but still, all the same, it's a little sad to be the only one left in the family. It will be a quiet Christmas, that's for sure."

Albert gazed out of the window as the train slowed on its way into Oxford, wondering how his sister would feel about him leaving, wondering what he'd do when he'd spent all the money, wondering what he'd do for Christmas Day. Something would turn up.

There were delays at Oxford while additional coaches were added to cope with the extra passengers. As the train pulled out around noon, George settled down to explain all the merits of narrow and broad gauge railways. Albert listened attentively and decided he liked George. He didn't really have a plan yet, but knew that George would be useful to him in Wolverhampton one day soon.

There was a screech. A sharp scraping of metal against metal. They both put their hands over their ears. They struggled to sit up straight. The train slowed, and their carriage bumped along the rough wooden sleepers. It rocked first one way, then the other. It lurched over and Albert clung onto the armrest of the seat as tightly as he could and cried out. It was like the day he'd been to the fair at Hyde Park. Jane had persuaded him to ride with her on the Ferris wheel. He hadn't liked it then, and didn't like it now. The carriage rolled and shuddered down the embankment. Seats shattered. Baggage fell everywhere.

There were deafening sounds of cracking wood, screaming people, shattering glass and heavy thuds. Wheels, seats and carriage doors all crumpled like a child's model thrown on the floor. Albert closed his eyes, waiting for the world to stop. Eventually it did. Silence for a few moments. He lay back on the cold but soft and white field, checking that his legs and arms were still intact.

"Mr Smith. George. Are you all right, sir?" Albert pushed himself up onto his elbows and saw George very close by, lying totally still in the snow and pinned under the beam from the roof of the carriage.

"Mr Smith. Mr Smith." Albert called more urgently as he pushed the beam as hard as possible and managed to relieve the pressure on George's chest enough for him to moan softly, still not opening his eyes. He was alive.

Chaos erupted all around. People screamed and shouted and others lay eerily still on the icy embankment. Albert continued to push up on the beam, listening to the soft cries from George and others nearby. He thought of Jane.

After an hour, two firemen arrived and helped Albert lift the beam completely away and put a dry thick blanket over George to warm him, before lifting him onto a wagon to take him back to Oxford. In the chaos and confusion, Albert was taken back in a separate carriage and never saw George again.

*

He couldn't help smiling at his luck. Albert looked around a room heavy with black wooden joists and yellowing walls, as the fire pushed out warmth and light. The roasted meat overwhelmed the pervading stench of stale beer. There were four tables, each with six diners, and Albert could see that none of them was a local.

Yesterday's events had brought some good fortune to the inn, and they had succeeded in finding the turkeys and vegetables in time for such a crowd, though he wasn't sure who was paying. No doubt the bar takings would be a big help.

"This is the most wonderful Christmas dinner a man could ever dream of." Albert smiled up at Milly as she put the steaming bowl of pudding and custard in front of him. "It's not just the food, it's the good fortune to be here, when I think what might have been. And a pretty smiling face to serve me."

"You just get on and eat, see. You'll need to be on your way soon, and I will be going home," she said.

"I know, I know. But a man can dream, you know."

Albert watched as Milly served the other diners, a crowded room buzzing with talk of the accident. The lady opposite spoke first on his table.

"It was the wheel apparently, it came clean off. Probably the frost," she said.

"There's over twenty dead, you know. Shocking, isn't it?" The man sitting next to him turned toward Albert as he spoke. "But this gentleman is the hero of the hour, aren't you, sir?"

"Oh, I don't know about that," said Albert.

"Well, by all reports, you are the one who held up that heavy lump of wood for over an hour, waiting on the firemen, trying to save that man's life. Well done – at least you tried."

Albert thought back to the conversations with George and his reasons for visiting Wolverhampton, and the inheritance. "I'd been travelling with him all the way from London. He was on his way to... well, to visit his aunt I believe. He died on his way to the Infirmary apparently; at least that's what the policeman told me when they dropped me here. A Mr Albert Paynter, he was. A proper gentleman," he said.

Albert glanced around the table, clutching his spoon of pudding, waiting for someone to ask him a question, feeling his face flush. Milly looked across from the bar. He met her eyes with a confident glare and a slight smile, and then he stood as he pushed the empty bowl away and wiped his mouth with the napkin.

"Excuse me, I think I need a little quiet," he said, as he walked over toward Milly.

"What are you up to?" she whispered.

Albert ordered another beer and watched Milly pour the pale brown liquid from the barrel into his jug. "I want you to run an errand for me, Milly. Will you do that? I'll pay you handsomely."

"What errand?"

"Well, the man who died. I know they have his jacket and bags at the station. I want you to collect them and bring them here, after you've finished work."

"Oh I have to go home. Mother is cooking our Christmas dinner, Albert. Anyway, why don't you go?"

"They'll probably recognise me. You can say you're collecting on behalf of the family. Perhaps his daughter or something, or you could be the family maid. No one will know or care, they just want to get rid of the stuff."

"It's stealing though, I'm not sure about that."

"Not really, he's dead. And he told me he had no family any more. None at all. So there's no one going to collect his things any time soon, that's for sure. What are a few clothes and cases? Probably not much in them anyway."

Milly finally agreed, but it took a small bribe that Albert didn't have. He gambled that there'd be some money in George Smith's baggage that he could share with Milly. Albert sat in the easy chair and listened to the idle chatter in the room as he gazed into the fire. He slowly nodded off, George Smith's bloody face staring back at him.

Albert stirred from his fireside nap when he heard horses and a commotion outside. The King's Arms dining room was quiet, the tables were cleared and neatly prepared for the evening meal. He walked to the front of the inn and peeped around the door to see what the fuss was about. Two men were lifting a large chest down from the cart as Milly held the horses still. They struggled with its weight and dropped it on the rough cobbles beside the window.

"Blimey, what's in there Milly?" The young porter at the inn sat on the chest and wiped his brow with his neckerchief.

"There's all sorts of belongings for some of the people staying here. It's from the station. There's a real crowd down there, you know. All just gandering at the train wreckage. Big pile of it in the station yard, there is. Engines, coaches, all mangled up."

"Well, looks like you found yourself a new scarf for Christmas, in amongst all those pickings."

"Oh, well, I… no. Look you, you just mind that chest. You'd think people would want to be with their families today anyway, not walking around train wreckage," she said.

"I guess it brightens up a Christmas afternoon. I'd love to get down there. How'd you manage to get the time off?"

"One of the guests asked me to go. Mr Pay..., I mean Smith. The one up in room 4. Seemed keen to get hold of his things today. I think he wants to move on tomorrow," she said. "Can you carry those two cases on the cart there – the brown ones with the 'Mr G Smith' tag. Take them up to room 4."

Albert pulled back away from the door so as not to be seen, and walked quickly through to the back stairs, to return to his room. Just as he shut the door, there was a knock and he let the porter in with the cases.

"Here you are Mr Smith. Milly said to bring these up to you straightaway."

Albert mumbled a thanks and showed the lad his empty pocket.

"Oh, don't worry, sir. What's it like being in a train crash, sir? You must need your rest and here's all your things. Looks pretty undamaged I think. Must be strong cases. It must have been exciting to see them tumble down the bank, sir."

"Right, that's enough. You can leave me to it."

When the door was closed, Albert put George's two cases up on the bed. He opened the first one, carefully pushing back the clasp and lifting the lid. There were sets of clothes that would keep Albert smart for years: jackets, shirts, ties, trousers, underpants, all neatly pressed and folded. Albert smiled and turned to the second case, just as there was a knock at the door and Milly rushed in without even waiting to be called.

"So, what have you got? Let's have a look," she said.

Albert pulled open the second case to show Milly even more clothes, but this time there was a folded letter lying on the top. He opened it and slowly read it out to her.

Dear Mr Smith,

We are very sorry to inform you of the death of your aunt, Mrs Mildred Smith.

Although I believe you have never met her, we understand you to be her only living relative, and in the terms of her last will and testament she has bequeathed part of her estate to you, the sum of twenty thousand pounds, with the balance going to charity. This money is available to you now, at our offices at the above address in Wolverhampton.

In accordance with our instructions, please bring the silver locket that belonged originally to your aunt. You father should have passed it to you before he died. It has a particular style, and we have a detailed description. This will prove your identity.

One further item, Mr Smith. In the terms of the will, your aunt is quite specific. In order to receive the money, you must be a married man. We assume that is the case and please bring your wife and marriage certificate with you to this office when you are ready to receive the funds.

Yours sincerely,
Bernard Asquith, Solicitor

Albert put down the letter and glanced up at Milly. Then he smiled and lifted up the small double-linked, heart-shaped locket lying next to the letter and without a word, he placed it around her neck and kissed her on the cheek.

Postscript

The official inquest for that Christmas Eve in 1874 concluded that a broken metal tyre on the wheel of carriage number 845 was the initial cause of the incident. It was the first carriage behind the two locomotives that were pulling the 10:00 am from Paddington to Birkenhead as it gently climbed toward Shipton-on-Cherwell, crossing the Oxford Canal. The icy conditions and the sudden braking of the two locomotives at the front before the guard applied the brakes at the rear exacerbated the accident, causing catastrophic derailment of all but four carriages.

There were over two hundred people on the train and most people in coach 845 did not have any chance of survival, as it left the track and tumbled down the embankment, rolling over multiple times and disintegrating. One of the other coaches fell into the freezing canal, breaking the ice. In total, thirty-four people died which made Shipton the worst accident on the Great Western Railway up to that time. One man was a hero, after holding up a wooden beam for an hour before firemen could rescue the trapped victim.

A Winter Lunch In The Cotswolds
Yvonne Hands

"This is the sort of Sunday lunch I look forward to," I said snugly to Bassily as we slid through the white fields and gently falling snow. "Gin and tonics and ancient houses sitting long and squatly on the streets of old Cotswold villages. And going inside and finding pale gold carpets and bowls of flowers and great wood fires and very smart people." I stopped, overcome for a moment with the picture.

"Better than the Christian Sunday lunch," I went on thoughtfully, "or even the University Sunday lunch, with hard settees and sherry and a very inferior roast ... No, that's not true," I said. "The roasts are often not inferior, but the settees jolly well are. And all the children looking on silently, and the conversation searching for a beginning, middle and end – particularly the beginning – and a slight smell of cabbage in the air."

Bassily said he thought that sounded very cheaply superior. Well, I thought, I'm not like that generally. I like the smell of Christian goodness, but on Sunday lunch, I quite like the smell of a decadent gin and tonic.

When we arrived at our hosts' house, it was indeed as I had thought. Pale carpets, beams and big wood fires and the smell of alcohol in the foreground – and distantly a pheasant casserole in the background. Altogether like opening a book and with the first line knowing you were in for a really good read, and settling down comfortably for blissful hours. When I arrived, I had to go up and do my hair. Another guest burst into the bedroom rather wide-eyed and dishevelled.

"I'll just pull my rollers out," she said, removing her scarf to show her hair tightly rolled up inside. She ran a casual comb through it, and was ready for downstairs. I rather gaped at her. Just the sort of woman I like. Hair all rolled up for the lunch party. Nothing wrong with that.

After two stunning G&Ts we groped our way through. The pheasant appeared, red wine with it. The conversation ebbed and flowed. The rollered-hair turned out to be an actress; she'd given up acting for the last two years as she and her husband had parted and she had to spend the time looking for another man.

"Any luck?" said one of the men with real interest.

"Not yet," she said casually.

I drank some more wine and ate my pheasant in an alcoholic haze, basking in this world outside my own. Its pale carpets and great sheaves of flowers, and through the window seeing ancient grey roofs, snow-coated, dipping to the ground, leaded windows turning their blank eyes on me, medieval chimneys. And snow-laden lawns and clipped hedges and the fields climbing up to a group of trees. And actresses in rollers searching for husbands. Nobody would ever be that honest in Oxford.

I told Bassily this as we were going home, how full of passion I was for that life. His mouth was buttoned down. He hadn't liked it. He hated pale gold carpets, a good strong red was the only colour for them. The pheasant casserole was far too rich, and he particularly didn't like ex-actresses feeling round his crotch while he was eating. Or actresses for that matter. His mouth buttoned even tighter, and I knew he had said all he was going to on that subject.

I began to smell the cabbage of future Sundays.

Sing, Choir of Angels
Birte Milne

The naked bodies of two lonely turkeys still waiting to be collected are all that remain on the long rack outside M. Feller, Son & Daughter. The Covered Market is still busy with people darting and hurrying in and out of shops. Any last minute shopper may just be lucky enough to get a bargain Christmas dinner if they hold their nerve for a bit longer. The cold gusts of wind sweeping up Avenue 2 of the Market carry along the tattered pages of a discarded newspaper and a piece of forgotten tinsel. Harry pulls his hat down tighter to keep it safe from the sudden gusts as he watches the necks of the turkeys sway in the wind.

"Fresh Cranberries. Last chance for your Cranberries."

"Free Range Ducks. Half price free-range ducks."

"Fresh Scottish Salmon. Best price in Oxford."

"Poinsettias and Hyacinths. Everything has to go."

Voices are calling from stalls all around eager to sell just a few more items before closing time. Harry watches the jolly shopkeepers with frostbitten faces banter with harassed customers, as red stiffened fingers wrap up the finest delicacies the market has to offer. Then he closes his eyes and breathes in the Christmas atmosphere of Nordman fir, oranges, stilton and coffee as they'd done many a Christmas Eve during the past forty years. Only this time Kathy is not there at his side when he opens his eyes again.

Harry walks slowly up and down the Avenues looking into every shop window he passes. The shops have changed over the years and he notices a couple that Kathy never had a chance to see. She would have loved Chocology and most likely spent a fortune there on those delicious Belgian chocolates if she'd had a chance, and she'd have been in her element roaming around Bangles to find just the perfect gifts for her girlfriends. Harry seeks out the comfort of some of their old favourites from years ago which have stood the test of time and are still going. John Gowing the jewellers, where they bought their wedding bands so many years ago and The Oxford Engraver where they had them inscribed, look just as they have always done. Harry rubs his thumb along the cold metal which still adorns his ring finger feeling the warmth of 'Kathy & Harry – Together Forever' against his skin. The Farmhouse where Kathy liked to buy most of their presents is bursting with gifts for every age and occasion. Then he finally makes it to their absolute favourite, The Cake Shop. The ladies are clearing away and busy cleaning up but give him a wave and smile through the window when they spot him. Looking at the amazingly ornate creations in the window he almost regrets not getting one of their small Christmas cakes. It would make the perfect 'last meal' washed down by a glass or two of the fine port from the flask in his pocket. By the time he gets to the door the lights are switched off and the shop is empty and he doesn't even bother trying the door handle. The port will have to do on its own.

The Avenues are now empty of shoppers and only the stall keepers are left rushing around hosing down counters and floors, packing everything safely away until Boxing Day before locking down the shutters. Harry lingers in the market for as long as possible as he watches the butchers, fishmongers, florists, stall holders and shop assistants leave with shouts of:

"Happy Christmas!" – "Have a good break!" – "Coming for a pint at The Tavern?" echoing under the high-raftered roof. He takes one final glance towards the meat rack outside Feller's where one last turkey hangs alone and forgotten, before making his way towards The Golden Cross and Cornmarket.

"Know just how you feel," he mutters to himself as he leaves the Market and the turkey behind.

The cold wind and sweeping rain beat down on the near deserted street. A few festive tunes ring out faintly from the brightly lit fast food restaurants tempting anyone still lingering outside to seek shelter and warmth. Harry walks quickly past, keeping his head down against the wind, struggling to stay upright as it hits him from all sides when he reaches Carfax. He stops for a moment to catch his breath in the doorway of Carfax Tower and feels his cheeks burn from the driving rain and cold. The empty waiting buses in Queen Street fill up in an instant from the queueing passengers eager to get out of the wind and home to their cosy, festive sitting rooms and last preparations. Harry wipes the wet off his face and pulls his hat firmly down before setting off again along The High towards The University Church of St Mary the Virgin.

They'd climbed the 124 steps to the top of the tower so often he'd lost count. The thrill of the amazing sight of Oxford's outstretched skyline meeting them at the top surprised him every time without fail; the way the view slowly filters through as they regain their breath. The last time – could it really be only six months ago since that beautiful June day? – he'd almost had to carry Kathy up the last few steps but they'd made it and spent a good hour just sitting, holding hands, taking in Oxford from above for the last time before making their way back down again.

"Promise me you'll keep visiting all our favourite places when I've gone," Kathy had said that evening. "I want you to go there as we have always done and talk to me about everything you see."

He'd promised he would. He'd never lied to her before but how could he tell her about the decision he'd made as they slowly descended the church tower together for the last time?

The rain turns to sleet and sweeps past him in wild flurries. At last the church appears like a picture postcard with its lights shining brightly through the stained glass windows into the fluffy specks of sleet swirling aimlessly in the dark afternoon. Harry pauses for a moment when he reaches the entrance to the church, wiping the water from his specs before casting a glance up and down the festive looking High Street. Then he gently turns the handle while pushing his right shoulder against the ancient solid oak door. It takes him a few seconds to realise that the handle isn't turning and the door is staying shut against the force of his shoulder. It's locked. The door is *locked*. He stares in disbelief at the bright fluorescent numbers on his watch. The time is 6.05 pm. Then he leans his forehead against the dark oak panels standing in his way, hardly able to control his despair at his own stupidity for not checking this crucial detail of his plan beforehand. Harry turns away from the door and steps back out into the piercing wind and scattered snowflakes. He needs to gather his thoughts and rethink his plan of action. He's come too far to turn back now.

The wind takes hold of his hat when he turns the corner of Catte Street. He makes an attempt to chase after it but soon realises he's fighting a losing battle against the merciless, unpredictable gusts sweeping across Radcliffe Square and abandons the pursuit. Thankfully he finds some shelter in the dark garden behind the church where he can recover from the snow, the wind and the major blow of the locked door. He searches deep into the coat for his hip flask and downs a couple of deep gulps from last Christmas's vintage port, sensing the warmth of the alcohol spreading slowly down his throat and around his cold, windswept body. The warming port calms his thoughts and despair and a new plan of escape begins to take shape: he'll join the churchgoers for Midnight Mass at 11.30. Once the service has finished and the congregation begins to disperse he'll quickly sneak away to the tower entrance and hide until everyone has gone. Then he'll slowly make his way to the top of the tower counting every one of the 124 steps in the light of his torch. When he reaches the top he'll embrace the view of Oxford's lights at midnight, describing the scene to Kathy in minute detail while emptying the last of his port. Then finally…

Harry takes another sip of his port, then he just sits with his scarf wrapped round his bare head, his collar raised around the ears and his gloved hands buried deep in the pockets of his coat. There in the corner of the doorway leading to the church vaults and garden café, motionless and unnoticed, cocooned by the darkness of the fierce night, he waits.

Kathy comes to him in his dream. His beautiful, smiling wife. His partner, lover, friend and soulmate. His everything. She is running barefoot through the tall grass towards his open, outstretched arms. They embrace and kiss. He feels warm, happy, safe and no longer alone. And as they run together hand in hand through the tall grasses, poppies and wild carrots of the meadow, the faint sound of deep organ pipes and a soaring choir of angels reach him from the far, far distance of the world he is leaving behind, through the bright stained glass windows of The University Church of St Mary the Virgin.

Young And Old
Penny Macleod

I have come to believe that the fateful moments of our lives are inescapable; they are simply destined to be. The time and manner of our death, for instance, is set in stone. And Christmas is like a portal in Time and Space in which experiences are heightened, more dramatic, because all is supposed to be goodwill. Goodwill is a tall order. So fateful experiences abound at Christmas.

The Great Quad bell rings out nine times. But there are no students scurrying through the quad today, late for their 9am lectures. I miss the buggers when they're away. I always do my rounds, even today. There's been no one to celebrate with since Mother died. We've had a film crew in the Hall shooting a banqueting scene up until 4pm on Christmas Eve, and it's no surprise to see that they didn't clear up the floor. Food debris all over the place. Let's take a look at the kitchen. Hello – why is the cereal vat here? They can't have served up Coco Pops with the Christmas banquet in yesterday's cinematic extravaganza. And here's a bowl with chocolate-coloured milk at the bottom; this cereal has been eaten this morning. Coco Pops smack of privilege – and someone who is still a child. And that is what my young friends are; they're just physically mature children. Clever, yes. But still kids.

It falls to me occasionally to play the detective. We've had the odd uninvited guest fetching up in the College during a vacation. It's an undervalued skill, being able to sniff out something odd going on in a large college like this. But I know the smells on every staircase, and in every Common Room. In the long summer vacation the place reverts to musty dankness; but the presence of just one intruder alters the smell. Out in the Great Quad now, I can detect something – it's the faintest tang of beer, appearing to come from the Junior Common Room. And there I find one of my young friends.

"Good Morning, sir. I'll just open these curtains up and let some light in."

"Oh, hello Partridge."

I take my time drawing back the curtains. It's his prerogative to expand the conversation, so I maintain a respectful silence.

"Hope you don't mind me camping out for a couple of days, Partridge."

"Not at all, sir. I shall enjoy it."

"Christmas is an over-rated festival."

"My sentiments exactly, sir."

He searches my face for a clue as to what I am really thinking, his thumb on the remote control for the TV, still switching between channels.

"I should imagine your family will miss you though, sir."

"We don't get on very well at the moment. Thought I might take a break from the whole family scene."

I nod to show him I sympathise.

"Tell you what, Partridge, why don't I accompany you on your rounds?"

"I'd be delighted, sir."

He makes for the door, letting the remote drop to the floor. For the thousandth time, I pick it up and turn off the TV. Youth.

"Been thinking about dropping out, Partridge."

"Really, sir? Is it the course you don't like?"

"Not sure. I'm beginning to feel I don't fit in here – or perhaps anywhere."

At last. An opportunity to engage with another human being going through a crisis. This is infinitely better than over-eating and drinking my way through Christmas Day.

"Is it the other students' supreme confidence, sir?"

"And their relentless pursuit of what they think defines them."

"Such as?"

"A rugby Blue. Membership of the Bullingdon. Shagging Olympics."

"You've had quite a change of heart, sir."

"What?"

"I remember you partying with the best of them your first term. And you were a roaring success in the College play last term."

"Lol, Partridge."

" 'Lol', sir?"

"Texting language – means 'laugh out loud'." He grins at me. "Do you really notice what all the students do?"

"Part of my job, sir."

"Bollocks. You're in charge of security of the College and re-directing nosy tourists."

"That also falls within my purview, sir."

He starts scrolling through the messages on his phone.

"I'll leave you to your phone, sir."

"No – don't go, Partridge. I'm not ignoring you."

He is texting, now, both thumbs moving over the tiny keyboard with astonishing rapidity. He speaks at the same time – beats me how they do that. How is it physically possible to hold two conversations – one written, one spoken – in your brain simultaneously?

"OMG."

"Sir?"

"Translates as 'Oh my God'. And the reason for calling upon the Divine is that my girlfriend is coming to check up on me."

"Not today, sir?"

"Yep – as in now."

"I'll leave you to go and get ready for them, sir."

Damn. Just when we were getting to know each other.

"No, Partridge! Sorry – I mean… Shit, I can't take her to my room. It's a tip. Her mum and dad are coming too, and there isn't time to clean up. Partridge – what am I gonna do?"

The alternatives go through my mind. No cafés open in town.

"Take them to a hotel for tea, sir?"

"No, they wouldn't like that."

There is another possibility. Unorthodox, perhaps. But I can handle it.

"I do have a suggestion, sir…"

And so it turned out that my young friend and I received Arabella and her parents by a roaring fire in the Tower. Professor Potter and his wife were currently sunning themselves in California, and I would ensure that the place was left spotless after our sojourn there. Unusually amongst academics, they were tidy and clean. And I was used to covering over a few traces. It was a luxury I allowed myself when they were away; I would spend a couple of nights in their double bed with a memory foam mattress, cook meals in their kitchen, read one of their books. And if the fancy took me, watch one of their films. One of the films they produce themselves, that is. Their interest in recording their unusual parties was safe with me.

"Hey – William!" Arabella bounces in, throwing her arms round his neck and kissing him. She leads him by the hand to the sofa, and snuggles up to him.

"This is super, Partridge," says Arabella's mother. "Such a cosy room – and one feels surrounded by history."

"It is indeed a special place, Madam." I take her coat. Her eyes inspect the room, registering Mrs Potter's collection of Lalique glass.

"It's sweet of you to bring us up here, William. What a treat." She flashes a smile at him that is only slightly forced.

"I was expecting a cold little garret room." Her father looks at me over his glasses, a twinkle of humour in his eye. "We used to freeze in the winter – no central heating in my day. Still, it kept the scouts busy, lighting our fires."

I allow myself to continue the conversation, as he has addressed this remark to me.

"Which college did you attend, sir?"

"Ah, well, I was at the 'Other Place'."

"I don't know why you went to Cambridge, Daddy. It's such a backwater."

He raises his eyebrows. "Always been one for the quiet life, sweetie."

Arabella perches on the arm of the sofa. Her flimsy chiffon skirt accentuates long creamy-white legs encased to mid-calf by fur-lined suede boots.

"You *so* have to come to our mega mega-bash on New Year's Eve, Will. It's gonna be seriously cool: five hundred guests, three different bands, a super-heated marquee just for me and my friends. You are coming, aren't you?"

"You do like parties, I hope, William?" Arabella's mother settles her gaze on him. I can hear the reservation in her voice, cloaked by her social skills. Every antenna is searching out his suitability for her daughter. Her eyes flicker for an instant.

"TBH, I'm not that keen on them," he says.

"TBH?" Arabella's mother enquires. I smile to myself, pleased that I'm not the only one unfamiliar with this confounded text language.

"It means 'to be honest', Mummy. Don't worry, William'll lighten up once he gets there," says Arabella. "And anyway, it's his duty to come and warm me up after my training exercise on Dartmoor."

"Yeah right." William sits forward on the sofa, extricating himself from his girlfriend's clutch. "Just don't expect me to join in your frantic activity, Arabella. I like to chill."

Arabella pouts; her mother raises her eyebrows. I decide to break the tension, and announce my intention to go down to the ground floor to replenish the log basket.

"I'll come with you, Partridge." Clearly Arabella's father feels the need for a break, too.

I open the door under the stairs and hand out logs to him. He loads them into the basket.

"Old Prof Potter would have a laugh if he saw me doing this," he says.

"You are acquainted with the Professor, sir?"

"We meet up from time to time on the conference circuit. I run a Management Consultancy firm. He's a bit of a media darling, as you know."

"He does get around, sir."

Arabella's father chuckles. I'm not aware that I have made a humorous remark. He catches my expression, pulls up to stand straight, and ignores the log I'm handing him.

"In terms of 'getting around', I've always felt that he and Mrs P sail a bit close to the wind, Partridge."

"Sir?"

"Come on, Partridge, I have a feeling that you know far more than you're letting on."

"It's really not my place, sir, to..."

"No, you're right, of course not. But I've always wanted to tell someone, Partridge..."

"You can confide in me sir. It will go no further."

"We go back a long way – the Potters, my wife and I. He had a bit of a thing for my wife. I never let it show, but I was actually quite upset by the, er, *attention*, he paid my wife at some of their more unconventional parties."

"I understand you perfectly, sir. I imagine I would have had the same reaction."

"Thank you. Feel better for telling you about it – you know – man-to-man."

We set off up the stairs with our basket, each taking a handle. We pause at the turn of the stairs to catch our breath.

"Not sure about that young man, Partridge. If he came to me for an interview, I don't know that I'd particularly want to give him a job. He seems to be a twenty-year-old going on about fifteen."

"It's my observation, sir, that many of today's young men are rather at a loss."

"How so?"

"They are being challenged by these confident young ladies who are such high achievers. And that leaves the young men feeling..." I search for the right word.

"Unmanned?" he suggests.

"Precisely, sir."

"I see your point, Partridge. Girls like my daughter, you mean?"

Alas, I am in deeper than I had intended.

"Your daughter is a remarkable young lady, sir."

"Takes after her mother." He winks at me, and we climb the remaining stairs.

Back in Professor Potter's drawing room, William hands out mugs of tea.

"William, do come home with us. You must be miserable here all by yourself." Arabella picks some imaginary fluff off his black fleece.

"Partridge and I can amuse ourselves perfectly well. But thanks for the offer. I'll think about it."

"We could drive you over to see your family next week."

"No – thanks."

Arabella's mother intervenes. "We must be on our way soon – we've got twenty people to lunch tomorrow. Do you think you might give us a little tour before we go, Partridge? I'd love to see the Hall."

We leave the young people on their own for twenty minutes. Twenty fateful minutes.

We returned to find William and Arabella in front of the television. They were intent on the screen. I recognised from the amateur camera work that this was one of the Professor's home-made films, featuring a highly bohemian party. In among the throng of writhing bodies a svelte woman and a well-known Professor disported themselves.

William's jaw drops visibly. He turns to look at Arabella's mother, then looks back at the screen, and sees the awful truth.

"Arabella, couldn't you have watched the Queen's Speech instead?" Her mother clearly takes *sangfroid* to new levels.

"Oh I don't know, watching you is much more entertaining, my dear." Her husband catches my eye. She ignores him.

"I wish we *had* watched the Queen's speech," says Arabella. She looks at William. She's apprehensive, waiting for his reaction.

William stands up, and goes to look out of the window. The other three people in the room sit in silence. William turns round to face the room.

"Well, it's been a pleasure to entertain you all," says William. "Partridge…"

"Yes sir?"

"It's like a light's gone on. In fact, I'm LMAO."

"Translation, sir?"

"Laughing my ass off, Partridge."

Arabella's parents finally look uncomfortable. William holds the floor.

"I realise that my family are unremarkable, but they are at least normal. I'm missing them. Would it be all right if…?"

"I understand entirely, sir. I'll take care of our guests."

"Thank you," says William. "And I'm sorry, but I won't be able to attend your New Year's bash, Arabella. Got to get my head down and do some work."

William crosses the room, and opens the door. He exits; doesn't close the door.

He calls back from the stairs outside: "Happy Christmas everyone!"

Schrödinger's Elf
Julie Adams

"I'm not going!"

The bell on the end of the curly-toed slipper belonging to the Associate with Responsibility for North Oxford tinkled as she stamped her foot.

"Now, be reasonable," said the Departmental Supervisor.

"I *am* reasonable," said the Associate with Responsibility for North Oxford. "I'm just not going."

"Look," said the Departmental Supervisor, "if you don't start getting ready right now I'm going to fetch the Vice President."

"Do that. See if I care." The Associate with Responsibility for North Oxford crossed her arms, the red and green sleeves pressed tightly against her woolly tunic.

The Departmental Supervisor narrowed his lips, weighing up whether up to continue the argument with the obstinate elf. He apparently decided he wouldn't and hurried off, the bobble on his hat bouncing from side to side.

He returned minutes later with the Vice President for the British Isles. The Vice President turned on his most oleaginous charm.

"Why don't you tell me what the problem is, my dear."

The elf bristled but said nothing.

"You know we have to get the show on the road in less than an hour, my dear."

"I am *not* 'your dear'."

"We have to pull together. Remember, there's no 'I' in team!"

Several elves had stopped working to listen and they nodded in agreement with the Vice President, chorusing, 'Together Everyone Achieves More'.

"What part of 'I'm not going' don't you understand?" asked the unhappy elf.

"Well, my de…" The Vice President looked desperately at the Departmental Supervisor for the elf's name.

"Twinkey," whispered the Departmental Supervisor.

"Well, Ms Twinkey, you're our representative in North Oxford. If you don't go, how will all those darling little children get their presents?"

"They're not 'darling little children'," said Twinkey. "They're all evil, scheming little …"

She was interrupted by a huge gasp from the watching elves.

"Now now, Ms Twinkey," said the Vice President. "We know that some are naughty and some are nice, but they all deserve to be cherished by our corporation."

Twinkey's nostrils flared.

"And to that end, we fulfil our mission statement: 'Every girl and every boy, gets a very special toy'."

The elvish Greek chorus joined in with him. The Vice President looked at Twinkey expectantly, but she just glared at the sack of toys marked with the OX2 postcode.

"I know what we'll do. We'll get you a nice cup of cocoa, and you can go and stroke the reindeer for five minutes. Shall we run that idea up the candy cane and see who salutes it?"

"You know where you can put your candy cane," muttered Twinkey. "Bent end first."

A few of the elves nearest to her raised mittens to their mouths to hide their sniggering.

The Vice President decided to try another tack. "We've got targets to meet, Ms Twinkey. Total Quality Enchantment."

Twinkey raised her eyes to the ceiling.

The Vice President snapped. "I might have to consider disciplinary intervention and competence proceedings for your dereliction of duty on Christmas Eve."

"I told you last year I wanted to be transferred."

"Why?" asked the Vice President.

"I've got my reasons," mumbled Twinkey, her bottom lip quivering.

"You'd better give me a good reason P.D.Q. Or else."

"Or else what?" she countered.

"Or else..." The Vice President looked around the workshop as if searching for the right sanction. "Gross Negligence of Obedience during a Merry Event!"

"Go ahead and G.N.O.M.E. me. Is this the face of an elf that cares?"

The Vice President knew he was beaten and issued the ultimate sanction. "I will tell," he paused, "The Boss."

The other elves gasped again. There were a few murmurs.

"Not The Boss!"

"You can't disturb him today, of all days."

Twinkey was too upset to feel threatened, and just stood there with tears coursing down her rosy apple cheeks. The murmuring continued among the assembled crowd.

"What's he going to say, being dragged away from Mission Control on Christmas Eve?"

"I wouldn't want to be in her curly-toed slippers at this moment."

They all became aware of footsteps approaching. Heavy footsteps. Everyone turned to look at the door. An enormous man stood there, hands on hips. Behind a bushy white beard his lips were pursed.

"Twinkey," he boomed.

The despondent elf raised her tear-stained face to him. The rest of the room held its breath.

"I haven't had an opportunity to say hello to you in a long time." He looked round for somewhere to sit. "Come," he said, patting his red-trousered lap. "Come and speak to me."

Twinkey walked over to The Boss, her head hanging. He reached down and lifted her onto his lap.

"You look after North Oxford at the moment, don't you?" he asked.

Twinkey started crying again.

"There there," said The Boss. "When you're ready you can tell me all about it." He produced a large snowy white handkerchief and gave it to Twinkey. "You can whisper it in my ear if you like."

Very soon Twinkey was able to start.

"It was last year, sir," she said. "It was the worst ever. They've done all sorts of things to me in the past. Like Eloise and Ewan in Norham Gardens; their father is a philosophy fellow. They tried to convince me I didn't exist."

The Boss smiled.

"And then there were the ones in Squitchey Lane whose mother teaches physics. They wanted to shut me in a box to recreate the experiment of Schrödinger's Cat."

The Boss laughed softly so that Twinkey was gently jostled by his huge belly.

Twinkey pushed out her bottom lip. "It's not funny."

"You're right, Twinkey," said The Boss. "But the children of North Oxford do tend to be a little advanced in some areas. They overhear a lot of interesting things and are shown the world in a unique way."

"But last year was the worst yet," continued Twinkey, tears brimming again.

"And why was that?" The Boss asked gently.

"The two…" She took a deep breath, "…lepidopterist's children, wanted to…" She swallowed, and the last few words came out in a long wail. "Pin me to a board and take me to the Pitt Rivers Museum."

Twinkey's body was wracked by gulping sobs. The Boss rocked her gently to and fro.

"Oh dear. This *is* worse than before. A few years ago in Davenant Road I had to put Ivan and Josephine on the naughty list for trying to map the genome of the family's cat. Very messy. Not nice at all."

His eyes softened as his gaze returned to Twinkey. "Have you tried to resolve this at all?"

Through her remaining sniffs Twinkey said, "I followed standard operational procedures and I visited the parents one night after the children had gone to bed."

The two senior elves nodded their approval.

"But," she continued, "their father took one look at me and shouted to his wife: 'Jane, the Little Green Men are back again!' and he ran out of his study."

The Boss thought for a few seconds. "Right," he boomed, slapping his knee. "I know what we'll do; it's too late to change the rounds now, so I'll come with you."

A murmur of admiration went round the room, and Twinkey looked up with hope in her eyes.

"And we'll give the children a taste of their own eggnog, so to speak."

Twinkey drew a red velvet cuff across her nose, not taking her eyes off The Boss.

"If the philosopher's children wait up for us, we'll remind them the anticipation of a thing is better than the thing itself. And in any case it would be impossible to accept presents from non-existent creatures. *Ipso facto.* Q.E.D."

Twinkey and several others giggled.

"As for the two junior physicists, we'll explain that as we are travelling at half the speed of light, Special Relativity theory applies and you have to allow for time dilation in the moving frame."

"How will Einstein help?" asked Twinkey.

"Then we follow up with, 'but motion is relative so who is moving – you or us? If I'm travelling at half of the speed of light and the children stay on earth, they might be too old to enjoy their presents once I arrive.' That should keep 'em quiet for a bit and they'll be grateful for whatever they get."

The Boss described the rest of his plan to Twinkey, then announced, "We've just got time for a snowball fight before we set off."

Everyone cheered.

"And we'll roast a few marshmallows."

Another cheer. Twinkey slipped off The Boss's lap and joined her colleagues as they rushed towards the door. The Vice President and the Departmental Supervisor followed at a more dignified pace.

The Boss called after them, "Last one to the North Pole is a scrooge!"

Both senior elves broke into a run, jostling one another as each tried to be first through the doorway.

The Boss pulled the double doors closed behind him as he left, saying, "Bah humbug."

The First Day
Jenny Burrage

Martha walked along Queen Street in a daze.

'70% OFF EVERYTHING'

'LAST FEW DAYS OF SALE'

'CLEARANCE SALE NOW ON'

Some of the signs completely covered the windows. She hated the January sales. Surely these goods were the things that hadn't sold. Why did people go mad for them? She hadn't come for the sales; her mission was different. She avoided the slippery lumps of ice on the pavements and made her way over to Costa Coffee for a cappuccino and a think. She had walked from Jericho and she felt tired.

Christmas had come and gone and her eyes had been so red and swollen after all the tears she could hardly bear to look in the mirror, but now the crying had stopped. Her parents had been very sympathetic and tried to make the Christmas weekend the best they could for her.

"Never mind dear," her mother kept saying. "You are well rid of him."

Her father was more forceful. "I'd like to get my hands round his neck," he said.

She licked the froth off the top of her coffee. What a fool she'd been! The bookshop where she had worked for the past fifteen years was the last place she'd expected to meet anyone who would look twice at her.

Here she was, Martha Jordan, forty-five years old and still unmarried. Of course nobody bothered about getting married these days, did they? Martha had hoped to marry one day, but then she was old-fashioned. She also thought of herself as not simply plain, but ugly. It was no wonder she was still single and had never had a lasting relationship. Now it didn't matter what she looked like. She would go it alone. What was that saying? 'Today is the first day of the rest of your life.' She absolutely knew it was for her. Things had changed now.

It was about a year ago that there he was in front of her, the man of her dreams. All right, that was a horribly corny expression but that was how she felt at the time. He was a rep who'd brought in a pile of children's books to sell. He was tall and dark-haired, and reminded her of Colin Firth exactly as the actor had appeared in 'Pride and Prejudice' some years ago.

She'd instantly liked the picture books he was offering, a series of stories for the under-fives about a family of meerkats. She had recommended them to the manager and that was the start of the friendship between herself and the rep, Jeff Reynolds. He obviously hadn't noticed her large nose and small blackberry eyes and clumpy legs.

He had taken her for lunch at The Nosebag on one of his monthly visits and Martha had invited him back to her place in Jericho the next time. She found out that even though he was thirty-six, he too was single and much preferred older women.

She was shocked when he told her she was beautiful. She had opened her mouth to protest but he had put his finger on her lips and taken her gently into his arms. Soon they were sleeping together and Martha looked forward to every day with a joyous feeling even if she wasn't meeting Jeff. Her life was meaningful. She had someone who enjoyed being with her. Jeff had stopped coming to the bookshop on business but still he was able to stay with her in Jericho when he visited Oxford.

Her flat had become alive now with the addition of rainbow-coloured cushions and vases of scented flowers. She scanned the internet for new recipes and prepared candlelit dinners for two.

She nibbled at the crunchy biscuit she had been tempted to buy and took another drink. She almost choked as she remembered the last time she'd seen Jeff.

"Come and spend Christmas with me and my parents," she'd invited him one evening in the middle of December, just as he was about to leave her flat.

"Love to," he'd said. "I'll text you."

She'd felt like dancing round the office when she got back to work that afternoon and couldn't resist telling her news to the manager, Graham. She hadn't told anyone on the staff about Jeff because he'd asked her to keep things secret, for the time being. She was convinced the younger ones laughed at her behind her back. They wouldn't have believed it would they? Martha with a gorgeous boyfriend at her age? She would have liked to tell them just to see their expressions.

"Always keep business and pleasure apart," Jeff had insisted, but surely it wouldn't matter now, especially as he never came to the shop any more?

"You remember that rep, Jeff Reynolds?" she'd asked when she was chatting to her boss in his office just before closing time. "I suppose you could say we're an item now and we're going to spend Christmas together."

There, she'd admitted it now to someone other than her parents and she felt good.

"Jeff Reynolds?"

She nodded.

"Have he and his wife split up then?"

"Wife?" She could hardly speak.

Graham frowned. "As far as I know he's happily married with a couple of young kids. His wife is the author of those meerkat books and she does the illustrations as well." He stared at her. "Sorry Martha."

She had relived those words in what seemed to her like every minute of every day since then. She was sure she would never hear from Jeff again. Today she didn't care any more. She didn't need him any longer.

She drank the last drop of her cappuccino, walked through the Clarendon Centre and crossed the road to Marks and Spencer. She felt suddenly light-headed and happier than she had ever felt in her whole life. Although the air was cold and a few snow flakes touched her face, there was a warmth inside her. She could feel herself smiling and what she was about to do made her hands shake with excitement. The store was crowded and she took the escalator up to the first floor almost leaping off as it stopped. She walked past the rails of women's clothes and shelves of shoes without looking at anything. She knew exactly what she wanted.

Later, after waiting in the long queue, she reached the counter. The assistant looked at the pile of baby clothes Martha had placed there.

"Aren't they beautiful?" she said as she folded a tiny pram suit and put it gently in a bag with the other things. "So tiny."

Martha smiled. "Yes they are... my first. I couldn't wait to buy them," she added.

For Old Times' Sake
Val Watkins

"For old times' sake," he had said.

It was a month ago today she had found it, New Year's Eve. They were going to a dinner dance at Oxford Town Hall. You had to dress up posh for those 'dos'. She had noticed a mark on the lapel of his dinner jacket after he had worn it at that business dinner in London, two weeks ago. She would have to sponge it now, as it was too late to take it to the cleaners. (Cleaners. She'd take him to the cleaners all right.) She got the dinner jacket out of the wardrobe and gave it a good shake. Something rattled and she saw a bulge in the pocket. She stared in amazement as she took out a glittering diamond choker. She could not speak. He'd bought her a present and hidden it in this jacket. It was a surprise gift for tonight. He was going to give it to her before they went to the dinner. What a wonderful, caring husband!

Stuff that! He'd never done anything like that in the whole of their fifteen years of marriage, had he? So whose choker was it? Had he really been to a conference a week ago? It wasn't that she trusted him implicitly. She didn't. She knew that he had his 'little bits on the side'. He'd go off once a week or once a fortnight, saying he'd got a 'conference on'. He'd come home all beaming and hearty, smiling to himself. He'd even popped off two days after Boxing Day saying he had a two-day conference in Scotland. Scotland my eye! She knew what he'd been up to – she wasn't stupid.

She didn't care. It meant she had the place to herself, tidy and clean without him messing it all up. He was a pain with his cigarette ash and spilling wine on her cream carpet, flattening her cushions and just generally making the place look untidy. She often shuddered when she remembered just before they got married how he had brought his big shaggy dog, a wolfhound or something ghastly, round to her flat. She'd been horrified at all the hairs it left around. It turned round suddenly and knocked her favourite

Doulton china statuette on the floor and smashed it. What did he do? Just laughed his head off.

"If you think we're having that thing in our new house when we're married then you've got another think coming," she said. "Get rid of it now. Take it to the Battersea Dogs Home."

He sulked for a week after that. They'd never had children either. She couldn't bear the thought of dirty nappies and toys messing the house up. He had wanted them, of course. But he didn't have to mop up after them did he? She often wondered if he had his 'little ladies' just to spite her.

But as long as he gave her enough money for housekeeping and spending on herself she had turned a blind eye to his 'women'. But a diamond choker! That was different. Had he bought it for a 'little lady' or did it already belong to one of his little sluts? Well, just wait till he got home tonight.

She heard his key in the lock, usual time – six o'clock on the dot.

"Hello dear," she called from the bedroom. "Your suit's up here, ready for you to put on and I've pressed your white evening shirt. I'm nearly ready, help yourself to a drink if you like."

"Yes, dear, I will. Up in a minute."

Duly refreshed, he made his way up the stairs and opened the bedroom door. She faced him, ready, in her black velvet evening gown. It had a low neckline and around her neck glowed the diamond choker. He looked at it and gulped.

"But that's Cin...!"

"Sin? Sinful? Yes, indeed. Sinful of you to spend so much money on me, dear. I found this in the pocket of your dinner jacket, so I assumed it was for me, dear. What a lovely present! I shall enjoy wearing it tonight, dear."

He sat on the end of the bed, a look of disbelief on his face.

"Oh, er, it's only on loan, dear," he stammered. "I haven't paid for it yet. I have to see if you like it. But it does look a bit heavy on you dear. Would you not like to try another? I can take you to the jeweller's the day after tomorrow and you can choose another, any you like."

"Oh no, dear, this is the one," she gushed. "You chose very wisely, dear. Shows how well you know me and my tastes. Now come on, hurry up, we don't want to be late. The taxi will be here at seven. The Morrisons will be wondering where we are."

He was grateful at the dinner dance that there was a cabaret after the meal and then dancing. He didn't have to talk to the Morrisons much. They had admired the diamond choker and she had been suitably flattered. He had smiled weakly and was very quiet during the meal. *Auld Lang Syne* at midnight, then – relief – they were getting their taxi and going home.

They got ready for bed in silence. They were in their beds (they had had twin beds for years) and she said,

"Well, who is she?"

"Who?"

"Don't treat me like an idiot. You know who I mean."

"If you mean the owner of the choker, it's Cindy."

"Oh, Cindy, is it? Well, I've put up with your little 'sidelines' for years but this is the last straw. She gets a diamond choker does she? More than you've ever given me! Tomorrow you pack your things and go to your precious Cindy. I've had enough."

"But …"

"No buts, we're finished. Good night."

"But listen…"

There was no answer.

He tried to talk to her again in the morning but she did not want to listen.

"Just go, it'll be a relief not to put up with your philandering any longer. JUST GO!" she screamed.

Half an hour later he trudged to the door with his suitcase.

"I'm going, dear, and er, can I have Cindy's choker back?"

A heavy glass vase veered dangerously in his direction. He ducked and raced to the porch. He managed to get out of the front door and close it just before a luscious pot plant orchid smashed into the back of it.

He rang. Several times. But she always hung up as soon as she realised it was him. He tried texting her on her mobile but she deleted it or wrote 'Get back to your tart,' in reply. So at last he wrote to her.

We must talk. I'm leaving the firm. There are things to settle. Meet me at The Old Parsonage on Banbury Road on Thursday. Please be there at seven o'clock, for old times' sake.

Well, she had to talk to him. Leaving the firm? After all these years! What? Had he gone crazy? Yes, she had to see him. He must be having a midlife crisis. What about her financial settlement and the future? This Cindy had turned his head. Perhaps he wanted to sort out finances or the house and contents. Perhaps he'd got another job. Well, she'd hired a solicitor anyway and she would indeed 'take him to the cleaners' as they say. She wouldn't let him talk her out of anything. She was going to keep the house – it was in joint names after all – and she expected a fair share of everything.

Oh no, she would not give in. She would show him. 'Cindy?' Huh! She'd show him what he was missing!

On Thursday afternoon she had her hair done at Mahogany. She got out her best navy dress and lovingly clasped the diamond choker around her neck. She then put on her black fur coat and called for a taxi.

She walked into The Old Parsonage just after seven o'clock. He was already there sitting at the bar. He offered her a drink and she asked for a Harvey's Bristol Cream. He got his beer and they moved to a table with comfortable seats.

Their conversation was very stilted. They talked about the weather, asked each other how they were getting on. At last she blurted out,

"What the hell are you doing, giving up your job? You must be mental! Are you going off round the world or something with your bit of totty? And what about me, you have to support me. I've got a solicitor. I'll see you in court!"

He looked at her wearily.

"Cindy is my Old English Sheepdog. She's been living with my mum for about eight years after Sammy died. When I've been away all those times I've been at my mum's, seeing Sammy, then Cindy, if you had only bothered to ask. Just before Christmas when I told you I was in London, I was in Abingdon with Mum. I took Cindy for a walk into town and saw the choker in H. Samuel. I took Cindy in and I put it round her neck like a collar. She wouldn't let me take it off. So I bought it for her."

He chuckled as he remembered.

"But later, I managed to get the choker off her and to hide it from my mum as I thought she would think I was going soft in the head. I put it in the pocket of my dinner jacket, which you had packed for me, and forgot about it."

She could not speak – dumbfounded was the word.

"The morning after when I bought my paper at the newsagent's I bought a lottery ticket for my mum and on the Saturday, when she checked the winning numbers, she found that she had won – seventeen million pounds! She has bought a farmhouse by the sea on the Isle of Skye. Cindy and I will live with her and mess about and do just what we want."

She snatched the choker from around her neck in disgust. Staring at him in disbelief she threw it after him as he walked out of The Old Parsonage.

Christmas Letter from the North
Birte Milne

Dear Holly,

I was a teenager when I met him. He simply swept me off my feet. He had experience, was always cheerful, full of surprises. He showered me with presents - and he had a wonderful way with children. I fell head over heels in love even though he wasn't a Brad Pitt lookalike - but he was lovely.

He asked me to move in with him. Told me he lived out of town - I thought Abingdon or perhaps Didcot but certainly not the bloody North Pole. Before I knew it, I was living in a gigantic house, miles away from Oxford and anything I had known before.

I miss watching Oxford United play at the Manor Ground, going to Bingo at the Regal with my mum and Aunt Carol and browsing round the market in Gloucester Green on a Wednesday afternoon. I think about our Saturday nights in The Turf, checking out the students before going clubbing in Park End Street. I dream about once again punting in the sunshine past the Cherwell Boathouse with a bottle of Lambrusco in tow.

Do you have any idea how cold it is here at the North Pole? But Clause, he loves it here. He shines with happiness when messing around with his assistants in the workshop. Me, I'm so bored, that one night I tried to teach the reindeer to play poker.

Every day is the same. Clause is busy in his workshop and I sit staring out the window. What happened to all my dreams? I wanted to do a beauty diploma at Oxpens College and now he doesn't even want to admit to everything I gave up for him.

He promised me the earth and I believed him. He's taken my best years - and I can't even get copies of Women's Weekly sent up here.

It took a long time before I realised that I'd never have him to myself. Something out there would always be more important than me. I've sat alone every Christmas Eve for the past twenty years. Who the hell can you ask to drop in for a drink and nibbles when you're at the North Pole?

I feel now that I've come to the end of my tether. Every evening is the same. He sits in his favourite chair, zapping away with the remote. All I get is "Shhhh" if they're showing 'White Christmas' or the 'Vicar of Dibley Christmas Special'. If I have to see Dawn French eat another Christmas pudding, I'll pull the beard off Clause. Never a chance for me to watch 'Inspector Morse' or 'Countdown'.

I'm so invisible that he won't even name a doll after me. When the alarm goes he gets up, puts on his clogs, grabs his sack and two minutes later I hear the sledge starting up. Never a kiss on the cheek or a hug - nothing.

I want you to know, I've tried. Seeing his large floppy belly hanging over the side of our double bed isn't really what I imagined I would have to put up with.

I'm ashamed to admit, I've had a fling with every one of his assistants, even the elf with the pointed ears, just trying to survive. But I can't carry on like this any more. People are talking.

Now he can go jump off a cliff! I've had it. I'm so angry and fed up. I want a divorce.

So I wanted to ask, Holly, if you know a good divorce lawyer? I think I must be entitled to half of everything after more than twenty years. Most of all, I want the sledge.

Hope to hear from you soon.
Love,
   Mary Christmas

A Different Christmas
Jenny Burrage

They all knew it would be there under the tree. It was always the last present to be opened. It had been for the previous five years, always the same thing, always the same murmur of 'thanks but no thanks'. After the flurry of present opening it had, in the past, turned out to be the highlight of the day, even for the grandchildren.

Sheila's pile of gifts had been opened already and placed next to her chair. They were always so thoughtfully chosen by the family. If she'd had to choose a favourite present, it would have to be a framed picture of her grandson Travis in his first year at school, his bright shining face smiling back at her. Of course there was still one present to come. Her heart skipped a beat.

She looked round at the familiar scene. There was a mounting stack of colourful wrapping papers in the middle of the room. The cards were strung about the walls on streamers and the holly popped in behind the picture frames. The Christmas tree as usual was nearly touching the ceiling, the glittering star on top almost having to bend over to stay in place.

"Mum, an artificial tree would be so much easier. They make brilliant ones these days. You can't tell the difference and there's no mess to clear up."

Lesley tried to convince her mother but Sheila couldn't be persuaded. She always went to the Covered Market for her tree and that was the way it was going to be. She loved the smell of pine and didn't mind clearing up the needles. Jack had loved it too. She sighed.

It was six years since he'd had the fatal car accident. He'd missed so much of their grandchildren growing up. Nicholas was now eleven, Holly eight, and Travis, who hadn't been born then, was five. She told herself to concentrate on what was going on and enjoy the celebrations. Stop it, stop it now, she thought. You can't bring him back. You've got to move on. The time was right for changes. She'd visited Jack's grave the day before and she had talked to him as she always did. She had told him her intentions and she felt better after that.

She could smell the turkey cooking and looked at her watch. It was time to go and inspect it, she decided. She insisted on doing the Christmas lunch herself with Lesley's help. Well it was still her house after all, the family home for over forty years, and she enjoyed being the boss in the kitchen.

"Your turn now Ma." Her son-in-law Steve interrupted her thoughts and pointed at the tree. "Best is always left till last," he laughed. The children stopped playing and stared at her. This was it, what they had all been waiting for.

"Just got to see to the turkey, won't be a minute," she told them. They groaned. She smiled at Arthur, old family friend and neighbour, who was sitting in a corner of the room. Dear Arthur, never far from her side. They'd been friends for a long time. How could she have managed without him after Jack died? He was always there for her and she felt sorry she'd taken him for granted. He had been so patient and it wasn't fair. This time it would be different. She'd made up her mind.

"Hurry up Gran!" Nicholas looked up from his Game Boy.

"Getting hungry?" she asked.

"No. It's just I want to see you open your present, you know the one you get every Christmas. That special one we always leave to the end."

"I can't wait to see your present as well," said Holly, "but I've had the most presents haven't I, Gran?"

"Yes you have and that's only fair," said Sheila, "for a Christmas Day baby."

"She's not a baby," Travis said. Sheila went into the kitchen leaving them discussing the unfairness or not of Holly's extra presents. They had the same family debate every year but Holly always won.

Sheila tipped the potatoes into the roasting tin around the turkey. She wondered how they managed to eat so many. Lesley put her head round the door.

"Everything OK, Mum?"

"Yes. Give me a minute or two please." She needed time to think before she went back in to face everyone and was given her present. She'd hardly slept last night. Of course maybe there wasn't one for her this year. She mustn't presume anything. It would serve her right if Arthur had changed his mind. She took off her apron, hung it on the back of the kitchen door and went into the sitting room.

As she sat down there was silence. The room had magically been cleared of debris and some of the toys and books moved aside. Travis came and sat on her lap and Holly sat on the floor next to her. Steve went to the tree, still wearing his Father Christmas hat with the dangling pompom. Then he stopped. He started searching through the branches, some of the pine needles dropping as he did so. Sheila's special present was always so small it often got hidden.

"Sorry Ma. There's nothing here, no more presents." Nicholas joined him, sure his father had made a mistake.

"Dad's right," he said after a few minutes' further searching. "No parcels, not even little ones."

The children looked at Arthur accusingly. Arthur looked at the ceiling. Holly put her arm round Sheila.

"Never mind Gran," she said. "You can have one of mine. You could have these blue beads." She unfastened them from round her neck.

"Thank you darling." Sheila felt a tear falling down her cheek. So… the ever patient Arthur had given up on her and she couldn't blame him.

"Wait a minute!" Arthur stood up. "I think there is something after all." He rooted around behind the armchair where he'd been sitting and brought out a large flat parcel tied with red ribbon which he handed to Sheila.

"Can I open it?" asked Travis.

"No Travis, it's Gran's special present," Lesley told him.

"Of course you can help me, Travis," Sheila said and she let him pull off the ribbon and the paper.

"It doesn't look like a box with a ring inside, does it?" said Holly, lifting off the lid and peering inside. "I think it's a box of chocolates."

For the last five years Arthur had presented Sheila with a small parcel containing a ring and a proposal of marriage, and every time she had refused him. His wife had died many years ago, quite young, and Sheila had never met her. Arthur's present to Sheila had become a ritual each Christmas Day since Jack died. He'd insisted she must keep the rings and she had them still in a drawer, unworn. The first three were diamonds and the last two had rubies and sapphires as well. She couldn't wear them because it would have meant she was engaged to Arthur and she wasn't.

I'm a sad case, she thought, but Jack's memory was always there. Even though Arthur had been turned down every Christmas, he had still persisted with the proposal and now it was too late.

"The box is empty, Gran." Nicholas had come over to look. Everyone except Sheila gazed at Arthur. Surely he wouldn't play a cruel trick like that? Sheila stared at the carpet. She was the one who'd been cruel.

Arthur came across the room and stood next to her. "Sheila I'm not playing games. I would never do that. I just wanted to do something different this year. Have a look in the lid of the box."

Sheila picked it up from the floor and turned it over. There was a message. The family were staring at her, wondering. She read it to herself.

Dearest Sheila,

I decided the ring idea was a really bad one. I still want to buy you another but I'd like us to choose it together. I love you so much and want us to be married. I don't mind whether we live in your house or mine or buy a new one. I'll even leave Oxford if that's what you want. Nothing matters except that we shall be together. Will you marry me this time?

All my love,

Arthur

Sheila turned to Arthur. "Thank you," she said. "It's a lovely message. Please would you read it aloud to me? I want to hear you saying it and the family can share it too."

Arthur took her hand. "I don't need to read it my darling. I know it off by heart." There wasn't a sound as he spoke, even Travis was still. Sheila kissed Arthur afterwards and whispered something in his ear.

"Gran said yes. I heard her," shouted Travis and suddenly the room was filled with cheering.

"Well done, Mum." Sheila hugged her mother and then Arthur.

"Congratulations you two. About time." Steve kissed Sheila and patted Arthur on the back.

"Can I be a bridesmaid at your wedding?" asked Holly.

"Can I come?" asked Travis.

"We're all coming, stupid," said Nicholas, "as long as I don't have to wear a suit."

Sheila laughed. "You can all do whatever you want." She grabbed Arthur's hand. "Come on you," she said. "Come and help me in the kitchen. That turkey needs some more attention if we're going to have anything to eat today."

Some Time Soon?
Neil Hancox

The rays of the low Christmas sun were reflected by the swathe of water separating the two Oxfords. The flood plain, between the east and west sides of the city, had triumphed over the designs of man. Charlie Edgar pulled his cap down to protect his eyes. Most of the trees were gone and the landscape had been re-modelled years ago so that he had a clear view from Iffley Church to the river. It was wide now. Later it would almost vanish and then, unpredictably, flood. The only constant thing was heat.

He wished he could savour real cold, maybe a little ice and snow, one more time, before his own time stopped. He took his battered pipe, packed it with tobacco, lit up and rested his body against a tombstone. He scraped away at the moss to reveal a date: 1851. There was nothing else. The soft limestone no longer held a name or an age. A nameless one had lain there for two hundred years.

Charlie looked across to the old church. That should last another century or two, despite the best efforts of the sun, rain and wind, though he had been told that the graveyard would be gone by the following week. The stone monuments would be removed, not with loving care, but as material to be recycled. The ground would be ploughed up, any bones raked to one side, and a crop of wheat sown to help feed the over-fertile population of this corner of England; too many people, that was the problem. In the future cremation would be the only option on death, unless one belonged to the governmental elite. There was always a patch of the precious soil for them. Charlie tapped his pipe on the stone angrily. He knew he shouldn't think like this. It was unworthy of his calling. Or was it?

Before he could solve the conundrum a voice called out, "Hello Charlie."

He looked up to see a tall woman. Sunglasses were jammed onto cropped blonde hair and her small hands and well manicured nails rested on her hips. He recognised the figure at once. He had known her since she was about ten years old, seen her through teen years and now into the beginning of womanhood.

"Hello Sophie."

She smiled, walked across and gave him a kiss.

"Let me introduce Phil," she said.

The man, about the same age, was equally tall and thin, with wire-rimmed glasses half hiding darting eyes. He was wearing a standard issue grey jump suit.

The new boyfriend, Charlie thought as he shook the outstretched hand. "You are in the border guard I see. Doing your three years?"

Phil nodded. "I started off in environmental hygiene," he said. "Two years at college. Now I'm doing the patriotic bit. It was either this or caring. It's OK. I'm stationed north of Reading."

"Do you get much excitement?" Charlie asked.

Phil shook his head. "I'm not bad at cards now," he grinned. "There's a bit of drug smuggling. Nothing serious. We have to stop some of our people trying to go north because it's supposed to be cooler there. Of course they don't know about the everlasting rain and ferocious hurricanes. And then there is the odd sun worshipper travelling in the opposite direction. The real problem is the south coast. People coming over the channel to escape the heat and everything it brings."

Sophie interrupted. "How are you getting on Charlie? I haven't seen you for a year or more."

"Saying goodbye to all this," he replied, "before it's used for food production, though the church will stay. That's something."

She nodded. "There's not much call for your line of work now, I expect, and we can't afford to waste land."

It was businesslike and what he would have expected from her. She had never been sentimental.

Phil slipped off his rucksack and produced a parcel and a bottle.

"Would you like to join us for an early supper Mr Edgar? Bread – real bread – cold meat and cheese," he said, "and," he patted the bottle, "this is rather good wine."

Charlie was amused by the archaic 'Mister'. Nowadays most people were a number, occasionally a first name or surname. The young man had some style. They laid out the food and wine and lounged on the grass. Afterwards Charlie wished he had not had any alcohol to drink. His head was beginning to ache. Maybe his pipe would help.

"Smoking is bad for your health," Sophie reproved him. "So put that away."

He shrugged and replaced the pipe in his pocket. The woman seemed more on edge than usual. Why had she come to see him today? Did she want to show off Phil and get Charlie's approval of her latest boyfriend? She could do worse. Charlie liked the young man and he might smooth off a few of Sophie's hard edges.

"Were you just passing?" Charlie asked Sophie. "Or did you want to see me for some reason?"

Phil became very busy collecting the scraps left over from their picnic, while Sophie hesitated. Charlie noticed a brief flash of colour in her face.

"I work in the social and environmental policy unit," she said as though this explained everything. "And I just wanted to see how you were," she added, but Charlie suspected that she no more believed that than he did.

They were all suddenly deflated. After a few minutes of silence Charlie pointed out the few bits of old Oxford still struggling to appear on the northern skyline. Most of the friendly roofs and domes had been replaced by people towers that prodded the clouds. They had to house everyone somehow and grow food as well. So *up* was the answer. Practical but not beautiful. Even worse if you lived there.

Phil worked his eyes over Charlie. The skin was burnt and wrinkled. Too much sun but that was hardly surprising nowadays. He must have been born in the last century. That made him old.

Charlie sensed the inspection. He wondered what stories Sophie had told Phil about him.

"I'll put you out of your misery," he said. "I'm eighty-seven. I was born when the world was cool, at least here. I eventually joined the church and I've been in this parish for thirty years."

Their reverie was broken by a distant roar.

"The midweek football game," Sophie said.

"It keeps the people amused," Phil added.

"Amusement," Charlie said. "We have enough to eat, even if it is usually a tasteless mush. Everyone has a small apartment with non-stop interactive TV, education is free, we live way past our sell-by date and yet most people are bored most of the time."

He paused, for breath rather than effect. "*Plus ça change.* Two thousand years ago the Romans kept the masses happy with bread and circuses, though I suppose they did tend to die young. Perhaps they were lucky."

He laughed. It certainly wasn't a conventional religious view. He must have been around too long himself.

Sophie turned towards him. She was angry. "Now we have everything we need. We live in the best possible world. We all know that, except, it seems, you."

She sat up, selected a pebble and threw it towards the church.

"What you are saying, Charlie, is rubbish. It's treasonable. If I hadn't known you for such a long time I would…" Her supply of words ran out.

"Steady on Sophie," Phil said, pulling at her arm. "There's some truth in what Mr Edgar says."

Charlie pushed his cap further down over his eyes to shut out the argument but the bickering continued. Phil showed some independence, while Sophie had taken the bait and swallowed the party line.

"I wonder," Charlie said to her, "if you'll become disillusioned like me? I believed all that stuff once. Well, most of it."

The girl was in control of her temper now. "What happened then to change your mind?" she asked.

"Reality kicked in," Charlie replied. "It's a nasty thing, reality. Politicians don't like it. Neither, to be fair, do the electorate."

"That's not a problem," the girl said. "Elections were abolished in the 2020s. There was clear evidence that they were not the best way for the ordinary people, with a limited understanding of the issues, to express their views, even when given the chance to vote again and again until they arrived at the desired decision."

She looked composed and serious and Charlie could detect no irony in her voice. It appeared that she had absorbed every bit of the party manifesto, and enjoyed regurgitating parts of it for the plebs. He yawned. He was tired and puzzled. This was not a casual visit. There had to be some purpose and he felt that Sophie had fluffed it. Let her go her own way. He was too old to probe any more

"Time I was off," he announced. "I have a service to take and a sermon to deliver, assuming I have a congregation this evening, about an event that happened a couple of thousand years ago in another sweltering country. They made a mess of things too. I suppose that's the human condition."

"Goodbye, you two," he called out as he began walking away. "Will you be coming along later?" he added as an afterthought.

Sophie remained silent and Phil looked uneasy.

As soon as he was out of earshot, Phil turned to the woman, "You were rather rude," he said. "And we didn't tell Mr Edgar what we were supposed to." His voice trailed off.

Sophie was silent. She came over to Phil and wrapped her arms round him. "I know. It wasn't what we had planned." She hugged him more closely and buried her face in his chest.

Charlie Edgar turned out the lights in the church. It was time to walk home, to his apartment – two rooms and poor soundproofing – and one of his interesting books.

The blast of cold hit him full in the face. It bored into his body in sensuous thrusts. He staggered, coughed and fought for breath. He realised that he had lost his glasses. His knees buckled very slowly. As he slipped to the ground he knew that this was his last Christmas and that his final wish had been granted.

"What did you do that for? You've killed him, I reckon." Phil fired the question and comment at Sophie. "You know we are only supposed to use that for self-defence."

She put down the small cylinder of liquid nitrogen and bent over the old man. There was no pulse. All that remained was to pull his cloak over the shrivelled face.

She turned to Phil. "It was the kindest thing I could do." There was no defiance in her voice. "If we had told him his church was soon to be demolished to make space for another people tower, that would have finished him and he would have died without hope."

Phil took her by the hand and they walked down the road in the direction of the next football match.

Winter in Oxford
Yvonne Hands

CIA Headquarters, Langley, Virginia

"Great," I cried. "Excellent. Winter in Oxford. Thank you so much for giving me such a marvellous present." I paused, overcome. After a minute I went on, "With all those arrogant Brits. Those dowdy, boring supercilious university wives, looking as if they are dressed in old dishcloths, condescending to this poor uncultured American. And to think I had booked to spend Christmas in sunny California, lying on the beach sipping cocktails. But, of course, I'll gladly cancel that."

I stopped, a broken woman.

"Pipe down, Agent Brown," snarled my boss. "We've been through this fucking crap of yours before. Ad nauseam. We all know what condescending little shits the Brits are, but remember this: your country's friends are your friends; your country's enemies are your enemies. Where you are sent is where you go. With your jaw clamped shut. Alternatively, you can fuck off now. Permanently."

"I'm irreplaceable." I arched my body, lifting my skirt in mock provocation showing stockings, suspenders and lace panties. I have found once or twice in my career, when all seemed lost, that lace panties got me out of a sticky situation (though into another, you might say). More useful than my gun. Sometimes.

"Keep your stock-in-trade for the poor suckers who don't know what a frigid bugger you really are," he snarled even louder, turning away – nevertheless taking a little peek before doing so. He hates it when I do this. So I do it every so often when I'm really pissed. Like now. Thinking about not lying on the beach. I've got great thighs, though I say it myself, rounded, soft, succulent.

He sat down heavily and joined his fingertips together, a sign of the deep seriousness of what he was about to say. "You are going to England. Something is happening there. We don't know what it is. But we know something's afoot. The feeling is that it's North Korea. And, if so, we have deeply got to be in there. At the front.

The feeling is also that the Brits could be playing one of their devious, underhand games. Personally, I think they are past it. Big time! Those days are over for them." He paused mid-sneer. "So, sort out those faggots in Oxford," he snapped. "And use a Canadian passport. Now fuck off out of my sight and don't come back till you've got the goods."

I duly fucked off; I always carry out orders. My last view of the boss for some months was typical, his eyes glaring, his mouth twisted ready to snarl. That's how he always looks at me. He loathes having to use me, he detests my approach, but for him the job comes first. I hate him and he hates me. He's one of those people whose job is their life. Made of iron. The only good thing about being in Britain is I won't have to see him.

In Oxford
So here I am, in jolly old Oxford, walking down the jolly old High, looking for some food that is not crap. Ah, found it: the Bank Hotel. See you later guys.

KGB Headquarters, Red Square, Moscow
"Winter in Oxford. Really." I remembered then to keep the elation out of my voice. "Winter in Oxford would be very inconvenient." I am now senior enough to say things like that. My boss just stared at me. Well, obviously not quite senior enough.

"When do I go?" I sounded extremely fed up at this assignment. It would be very unwise to let them think I wanted to go. My boss looks like a pig. He is a pig. I hate pigs. He explained that something is afoot in Britain. They thought Oxford. There wasn't much to go on, just a general feeling. The feeling is that it could be North Korea. If so, we absolutely had to be in on it. We must take the lead in this. He didn't trust the British. Devious buggers. Always have been. He thought it unlikely, he felt their days of pulling the strings in the background were over. But I was to go and find out. And come back with the goodies. Otherwise, not to bother to come back. His small eyes, over his pig-like snout snarled a message to me. That's just what he would like. Right, I took it. He really resents having to use me, he feels I'm too effete. But obviously, right for this.

I looked through the window of his office onto Red Square. The snow fell softly against the window frame, white against the Kremlin red brick wall. One of the great views of the world. But I was seeing ancient grey stone walls, crooked doorways, famous bookshops. Tea shops, where English ladies sipped from delicate cups. The greatest cultural city in the world. I could hardly contain my joy. Of course, I showed none of this.

I walked back to the general office and looked at my colleagues pityingly. They were not chosen. They looked back at me. Expressionlessly. That was the thing these days, the Putin Look. The poker face. Showing nothing. Putin had been a KGB man and made it to the top. So now, His was the face. It looked rather strange on two of my colleagues who were Tartars and by nature had the expressionless high-cheekboned slanting eyes of their people. Putin sat rather oddly on top of that. Oxford! I turned away to hide my delight. I had been in the KGB for over twenty years. I have done all the things that have to be done, in that position. Done more than most, and have been recognised as such. I am one of their most senior and trusted men. Therefore this assignment. In the last years I have found myself changing. I want to live a different life. Gentler. I would like to study. Of course, I cannot say this. I go on as before. But the thought of living in Oxford for a time filled me with joy.

Oxford

Here I am, to my delight, walking down The High – that is what it is called. Not 'High Street' but 'The High.' How very Oxford. I am passing a lot of delicious-looking little restaurants and cafés. But I am facing one called 'The Bank Hotel'. I'll go there. The place is very full, only one empty seat. I ask the lone lady if I may share. She acquiesces. She tells me she is from Canada. She is doing some research for her university. Really, I say, so am I. From Krakow University, I tell her. (I travel as a Pole, it's easier.) We fall into conversation over the meal and compare notes.

New Year's Day, on the plane back to Washington

What a way to spend New Year. The whole thing a waste of time. The same old condescending dish-cloth clothed wives. Bemoaning the fact that we dragged them into the Iraq war. Who dragged who into the European war? The same red-faced Englishmen, never saying what they mean.

Well, I snooped round Oxford. I was loaded down with introductory letters to all sorts of people – the CIA is very good at that. I sat in libraries doing my phoney research. I went to endless college dinners, sitting at high table with the dons. I was designated one particular college. Believe me, I really worked at it, and everyone there. I snooped, sniffed, nuzzled, smiled, charmed, but could find nothing. I got on particularly close terms with the head of the college. Some damn name like Warden or Master. When I say 'close terms', I mean as close as I could. Peregrine, his name was. Peregrine! Christ, what a name! I had dinner with him a lot of times. A particularly idiot Englishman (the home of idiots). Had dinner in his rooms. So desperate was I to get through I once had to fall so that my skirt came right up to my waist (a trick of mine) and showed all, panties, the lot. He didn't even notice, went on talking and guffawing at his own jokes. Ho, ho, ho! He's a widower and lives alone. I don't think he knows what women are. Went to the right English public school obviously. Probably can't get it up. Except when they play 'God Save the Queen'. Then the trouser buttons hit the ceiling. When I was leaving I went to see him. He was just having a Chinese takeaway delivered by a Chinese guy. Can you imagine, the food is so good at that college, they have to have takeaways? I left him guffawing and chuckling in an idiot fashion. Even my boss seems succulent after him. I'm taking my vacation now, whatever Dear Old Boss says. Lovely hot Californian beaches. Cocktails! No more idiot men. Yippee!

New Year's Day, on the plane back to Moscow

What a sad way to spend New Year's Day. Going back to Moscow. I feel a different person. I know I will find the crudeness of

Moscow hard to take. What a great time I had. What wonderful people. How kind, how cultured.

I was given many letters of introduction (the KGB is very good at that) and so met a great many interesting people.

I grew very close to the head of one college (the college I was designated to look very closely at), Sir Peregrine Beresford-Montague. What a marvellous name. A very simple kind of man, sympathetic, but not really of this world. A real Oxford academic. Far too honourable to be involved in dirty political practices. When I went to say goodbye, he was having a Chinese meal in his rooms, with an old Chinese friend. Very informal and cosy. Old friends together. I would have loved to stay there with them. I hope one day to go back and do some studying there. He has become a father figure to me and said he would help me to do that. Happy days.

A College Room, Oxford

Sir Peregrine talks to his guest, an envoy from North Korea.

"Well," said Sir Peregrine thoughtfully, chewing somewhat reluctantly on the Chinese dishes delivered by his guest. "I think we got away with it. A near shave once or twice. With the KGB and CIA hanging around I thought they had sniffed us out. The CIA girl is supposed to be one of their best. I didn't think her so bright."

He chewed on, reflectively. "Rather jolly knickers, though."

Christmas Presence
Dion Vicars

Christmas Eve

It's approaching 3 o'clock and the shops are beginning to close. Only the most avid bargain hunters remain. Dad is still searching for some last-minute jokey presents for the family. The market has yielded a catnip mouse for Tiddles, Boswells a gingham apron for the daughter and very nearly a plaster cast thatch cottage for Mum. But not quite.

The Works, opposite, beckons with their usual banner 'Everything Must Go!' Searching through the array of huge discounts he notices *Fridge-ffiti*, a set of magnetic fridge letters in wacky fonts and it's just right. One more is needed for his anthropologist son and the museums seem a likely possibility. The University Museum itself has mostly dinosaur models and posters, but the Pitt Rivers Museum at the far end is an Aladdin's cave.

He is attracted by the red 'Reduced' label on a replica crystal skull. It is absurdly kitsch with an LCD thermometer disc in one eye socket and a barometer disc in the other. One of them is reduced from £10.99 to £5.50 because of a slight impurity in the plastic. It's two minutes to closing time and everything is cashed up. Adroit application of market forces gets it for a ready fiver.

Christmas Day

"Well, William Hill won't have lost any money."

It is grey and raining outside, but the fire is alight. They have a minimal breakfast so as to leave space for dinner. Some concerted family effort has the preparations for the meal completed by eleven. Time for a drink and the fun present opening as a warm up for the bash after lunch.

Tiddles comes in through the cat flap, soaked, and finds a bare leg to rub against. He is scooped up and dried with a tea towel and much purring.

They adjourn to the living room where the tree is alight on a mound of presents, trivia presents clearly on one side. Tiddles notices something in spite of the hermetically sealed wrapping, so he gets his first and is ecstatic. Inhaling the scent of the catnip and trying to get all four paws on it at once, eventually he subsides and retires to his favourite place under the sofa which traps the heat from the fire.

Now for theirs. Jane first. She gives it a good feel over, none too sure what to expect, and fortunately is pleased by the apron. Dad gets a remote-controlled helicopter, Mum the *Fridge-ffiti* and is delighted. Then Andy. He opens the small heavy box.

"What's this, Dad?" He takes out the skull and laughs. At first.

"Is this really plastic? It seems more like crystal or possibly quartz." He notes the 'Reduced' label Dad has forgotten to remove.

"I should have known!" He inspects it.

"What's in it? It looks like bubbles. One of them is reflecting the fire."

"The barometer bit isn't much good – it's showing 'Fine'. The thermometer isn't much good either; it's showing 28 degrees. Has it been on the radiator?"

Andy takes a more detailed look. "I think this is Central American. Does it say anything on the box?"

"No, just the description."

"Have you got a present for it, Dad? A little Christmas hat and beard perhaps?"

"Later on maybe. Let's see what's in the crackers."

"Oh well, it will look good on the hearth," and he puts it there.

"OK, let's have a go at the 'copter."

They get it out of the box and the women leave for the kitchen.

"How's it work? Infrared isn't it?"

They take goes at flying it.

"Hey Dad, the controller makes something in the skull glow – it must pick up the infrared. Let's try it with the TV controller."

They turn on the TV and select a channel. The crystal skull does seem to respond to it. A picture comes up on the screen. It is of a forest as far as one can see, with a stepped pyramid in the centre and a clear way leading up to it. The sky is clear and the sunlight is strong.

Andy says, "Oh no! Not 'Star Wars' again."

Dad says, "I don't think it's on." They check the Radio Times. "No, it's not."

Andy says, "I think I recognise it, Dad. It's Tikal, where we had the field trip last year."

They try another channel and get some carols, but then there is a call from the kitchen to get ready for dinner leaving the TV on standby. In the kitchen Jane is wearing the apron and there is already some of the graffiti on the fridge:

BOYS
TOYS
GIRLS
CURLS

and:

IF I GIVE MY HEART TO YOU?
WILL YOU GIVE ME ALL YOUR LOVE?
WILL YOU SWEAR THAT YOU'LL BE TRUE?
BY THE LIGHT THAT SHINES ABOVE?

Dad says, "So the gingham has kicked in, Jane. Dean Martin isn't it?"

Jane says, "No, Dad, it's Doris Day. Goes with the apron – right?"

Dinner Time

Dinner is readied and served. By consensus, no bird this year but prime organic fillet steak from Alcocks.

Now that the children have left home the cat has gained more space and licence. He sits on one of the work surfaces when they start the meal.

Mum says, "He thinks he is one of us – he likes to be on our eye level."

Jane says, "For God's sake, Mum, you can't let him sit on the surfaces – it's not hygienic."

She lifts him off the surface, puts him on the floor and wipes the place with a J-cloth. Tiddles is unamused, not to say miffed. He gives the assembled company a disdainful glare and exits through the cat flap into the gloom.

The dinner goes well. Dad is ribbed about his toy and the 'Reduced' label. Mum has more ideas for the *Fridge-Ffiti*. This has plainly opened up a whole new channel of communication. Jane has already used the retro apron in earnest while preparing the dinner.

They are catching up with each other about their activities over the last three months when the sound of the TV is heard. It is the sound of chanting and drumbeats. Dad goes into the living room and the telly is indeed on and showing the same picture of the forest and pyramid, but now there is a group of people, some in gold-coloured robes, processing in a line towards the pyramid, chanting. He turns it off completely and returns to dinner.

The Christmas Pudding is lit and consumed. The crackers and their jokes cracked. Coffee is prepared, chocolate unwrapped. Tiddles returns, damp again, is duly dried, then goes to the living room warmth and catnip mouse.

Present Giving Time
They take their coffees into the living room and would like to have a single round of present giving before turning the TV on for the Queen's Christmas message, but there isn't time so Mum chooses the whole-family present from Andy. It is a big box which rattles.

Dad thinks, "Must have taken an acre of wrapping paper."

Mum is the champion on recycling wrapping paper but tears this too much because of the rush. Turns out to be a new game called Cranium – 'The Act-it, Draw-it, Sculpt-it Game for all the family' it says on the box.

But first the Queen.

The TV takes a moment to warm up but it is showing the same forest scene. Now the people in the picture are close to the pyramid. They are led by a woman with long, black hair down her back, holding a staff, dressed in a gold robe and chains with a long gold train held by two girls. She is followed immediately by four people borne on stretchers held high, each accompanied by an attendant with a gold tunic. The large crowd of people is chanting to an insistent drumbeat. The sky is still clear but the sunlight is not so strong.

Dad says, "OK. We don't want this."

Dad takes the controller to change channels. It has no effect on the TV, but it does on the skull: with each button press the red glow within it gets stronger. Finally, in exasperation Dad decides to turn it off, but with no apparent effect. It stays on and the crystal skull suddenly radiates a searing white light, though still with the red in the centre.

From their seats on the sofas they are gripped.

They want to look away but can't.

They want to get up but can't.

They are paralysed where they sit, forced to watch the spectacle unfolding on the TV screen.

*

The leading woman ascends to a seat at the top of the pyramid followed by the four people who are laid on four waist-high slabs with their attendants standing beside them. It is now evident that there are two women, one of them young, and two men, one of them also young. They are wearing little but are covered with gold sheets.

The woman on the seat is watching the setting sun. As it touches the horizon, swollen and orange, she lifts a baton and hits a drum. The drumbeat intensifies and suddenly stops.

At that moment all four attendants take out knives and stab into the sacrifices, removing something large and dark red. They all turn towards the setting sun offering their trophies. As they do so something translucent near the woman's seat catches the setting sun, giving out a strong white light, subsiding into a slowly throbbing red glow.

*

Tiddles is disturbed under the sofa when the TV controller drops onto the wooden floor making a loud clatter, hitting and moving the catnip mouse.

'*Ha! It moved.*' He leaps on the mouse and hits it to the other end of the sofa. '*Ha! It moved again.*' He jumps on to it, skidding on the polished floor.

He continues the important business of chasing the elusive mouse round the living room, ignoring such trivia as the Queen talking on the television, the satisfied pulsing red glow from the crystal skull on the hearth and the four lifeless red-soaked forms on the sofas.

Miloria's Big Performance
Val Watkins

Jennifer Stubbs had always wanted to be a ballerina. From being a plump, dimpled four-year-old, plain Jennifer longed to wear a white tutu with layers of snowy, floating tulle. However, she was overweight and this proved a barrier to success in ballet lessons. The more she dreamt of being 'Miloria Valashnikova, the great ballerina, starring in *Swan Lake* at Covent Garden', the further away from possibility the dream became. All that remained was her name. She became Miloria Jennifer Stubbs.

When Miloria started working at Dorkham and Jollybody's (*'Oxford's most customer-friendly department store'*) at the age of seventeen, she was determined to succeed. She was now, at the age of twenty-two, a very efficient Deputy Manageress of the large toy department, which was situated on the fourth floor.

Miloria spent a lot of her leisure time in the local library near her home in Summertown, where she lived with her parents. She lost herself in books about great ballerinas, such as Alicia Markova, Margot Fonteyn and Darcey Bussell. On Saturdays she would go to see a matinee film or a ballet with her friend Daphne who lived two doors away from her. Daphne was quiet and retiring, spending her time knitting sets of woolly hats and matching long scarves of which Miloria had twelve.

The Manager of the toy department was Mr Harold Applewhite, thirty-two years old, tall, brusque, his immaculate dark hair swept back. He ran the toy department meticulously; he knew what was happening on every shelf, in every corner, and in every cash desk. No slacking was allowed. Thus the sales figures for toys were the best in the store and had been for the last six years. At first Miloria simply eyed him with awe and admiration but recently, since she had been promoted, she saw him through more romantic eyes.

During the last few months a gang of shoplifters had been targeting Dorkham and Jollybody's, and thefts were occurring in all departments of the store. This was making Miloria very nervous. There had been no clue as to the identity of the thieves but the crimes were obviously being perpetrated by a set of clever criminals. The losses to the firm were heavy, and the directors were dreading Christmas approaching and the chaos that this would bring.

As usual, the toy department staff met to discuss their Christmas campaign, planning every detail punctiliously. The highlight was to be 'Santa's Grotto' at the far end of the department. Icicles and glittering snow were to be spread over Santa's large igloo-shaped grotto in the midst of a snowy, tree-laden landscape, with sparkling silver stars hanging from the white coated ceiling. The wide-eyed child would enter, meet Santa and receive a present. Mr Jackson was appointed to his usual role of Santa Claus, which he had fulfilled for the last ten years. Then Mr Applewhite announced,

"All departments are struggling with staff shortages and none of the juniors is available to be a fairy. There is only one thing for it, Miss Stubbs, you must be our Fairy Twinkle!"

"Oh, I c-couldn't possibly, Mr Applewhite!" Miloria stuttered. "It's not my er…"

"Oh, come on, Miss Stubbs, you can do this. You know all about dancing. Consider the prestige that this new addition to Santa's Grotto will give to the best toy department in Oxford!"

"Oh, if you put it that way, Mr Applewhite…" Miloria was stunned but secretly thrilled – Mr Applewhite had chosen her!

Mr Applewhite continued, "I'm sure you could rustle up a costume with some material and sequins or something from the drapery department. You could run it up yourself quite cheaply. We must keep costs to a minimum."

"I've heard of these electronically driven twinkling wands that can be switched off at …"

"Oh no, Miss Stubbs," Mr Applewhite said hastily, "we can't afford luxuries like that! A piece of dowling painted silver with a cardboard star on the end will have to suffice. Go through the usual channels with your expenses. Now for the next item on the agenda: please be vigilant at all times, it would be good for our reputation if we could catch the thieves who are currently causing havoc..."

Miloria was ecstatic, her mind full of plans for her fairy costume. The next day she went down to the drapery department and found some white netting, some white viscose lining material and a bag of silver sequins. She went home that night and planned her costume. There was enough material for the dress to be calf-length and she got out her sewing machine and started straight away.

Miloria still hankered after an electronic wand with twinkling lights. She knew the firm of electricians that Dorkham and Jollybody's dealt with, Connectus Electronics of Cowley. They were always very obliging about any electrical work that needed doing in the toy department. She rang Mr Bright, the departmental manager and skilfully negotiated a free wand in exchange for a display advertising his company.

A few days later Mr Lightham, head electrician at Connectus Electronics, delivered a wand – a long silver tube with a twinkling star on the end. Its lights would go on and off intermittently. He brought the finished wand to the Toy Department the following week to test it.

"It's wonderful, Mr Lightham," enthused Miloria. "Many thanks. I am so grateful." She waved the sparkling wand in the air.

Mr Applewhite looked on and was most impressed with Miloria's ingenuity and initiative.

In the evenings Miloria toiled away at her dress. In the daytime she breezed serenely around the department, dealing with staff and customers as efficiently as ever.

"Wayne is only seven," said a bristling mother, presenting Miloria with her son's Megazord Transformer. "How is he expected to understand instructions in Japanese?"

"I am so sorry, Mrs Perkins," soothed Miloria. "I'll just sort this out for you." She found a spare set of English instructions and gave them to Mrs Perkins.

"Why they can't put them in the box in the first place I don't know," grumbled Mrs Perkins. "I've had to come all the way from Abingdon."

"I do apologise," said Miloria. "May I give you our special ten pound voucher towards any toy in this department? You may spend it any time before Christmas. As you know, Mrs Perkins, we value your custom greatly."

Mr Applewhite, standing discreetly behind The Incredible Hulk display, nodded approvingly.

At last the dress was ready. Miloria looked at herself in the mirror. It fitted perfectly. She hummed 'The Dance of the Sugar Plum Fairy' as she twirled and swirled. She had made a little tiara out of wire, silver foil and sequins and she had found a pair of white ballet shoes.

The first day of December arrived and the toy department staff assembled for the momentous opening of Santa's Grotto. Mr Jackson was ready in his Santa suit with a flowing white beard, the hairs of which kept getting in his mouth.

Miloria dressed in the staff ladies' toilets then stepped into the Grotto and did a twirl for the staff in her outfit with her twinkling fairy wand. She stepped up on to her toes in her satin ballet shoes and waited for the applause. There was a startled gasp and Mr Applewhite said,

"Ah, Miloria, you look, er, very nice."

There were sounds of children and mothers and fathers approaching as Miloria took her place beside the Christmas tree and repeated her twirl. After they had had their chat with Santa there were a lot of children with very happy faces as they went away clutching their presents, the boys with blue, shiny parcels and the girls with pink.

At the end of the day Mr Applewhite was very pleased. The takings were well up on the year before.

Later in the month, a gang of shoplifters met in a drab old garage off the Iffley Road.

"Right," said their leader. "We've been doing very well this last few weeks at Dorkham and Jollybody's. Serves them right for giving me the sack from their warehouse. It's time to step up the thefts. I can get rid of a lot of gear to outlets wanting stuff for the Christmas trade. We'll continue working in twos: CDs, DVDs, iPods, calculators, mobile phones, watches, toys, radios, the sort of stuff that sells well and isn't easy to trace. You all know the routine."

The next day two of the gang, a dark-haired, short, stocky teenager in a blue, elasticated jerkin and jeans, and a tall, thin man in a black duffel coat and combat trousers ambled along to Dorkham and Jollybody's. They looked at the store's floor indicator for *Music Department* and took the escalator up to the fourth floor. As they walked through the toy department to the music department they noticed a queue of children with mums and dads milling about.

"Oh, blimey," the thin man said. "It's a Santa's Grotto, all the little darlings are queueing up to get their presents. Ain't that sweet? And what the 'ell does that woman think she's doing in that ghastly frock, waving that stick around? She'll whack somebody in a minute."

They tittered as they passed Miloria. They walked through to the music department. It was busy with shoppers looking for Christmas presents. There was only one assistant at the counter by the cash register. He was concentrating on a customer who was complaining about a scratched CD. The rest of the staff must have been on tea break or in the stockroom. The thin man walked over to the DVD film racks. He looked at the titles quickly; all the latest releases were there. He rearranged them surreptitiously on the stand in two piles of two. Then he wandered away and stared busily at the Bang and Olufsen hi-fi display nearby. The sole member of staff was looking at the customer's CD closely. There was a queue waiting to pay. The teenager walked quickly over to the DVD racks. With both hands he scooped up the four DVDs, stuffed them into his elasticated jacket and walked casually through the music department, the thin man joining him. They were nearly at the toy department when a high-pitched cry went up. A little old lady was shrieking and pointing with her umbrella.

"That boy, he's taken your DVDs! Catch him!"

Like a flash the assistant dropped everything and ran.

"Stop, thieves!" he yelled. "Stop them! Stop them!"

By now the two thieves were charging through the toy department amongst the children and their parents. Miloria, on her twentieth twirl of the day, turned and saw them hurtling towards her. The two men looked pretty ugly and threatening but Miloria closed her eyes, stuck out her twinkling wand and tripped the teenager up. There was a flash and the sparkling lights all went out.

The music department assistant, several children and mums and dads all fell on top of the teenager and the thin man and they were well and truly floored! The store detective soon arrived and the two of them were taken to Harold's office to await the arrival of the police.

Miloria stared dejectedly at her wand. Her tiara sat crookedly on her head. She looked dishevelled and her dress was dusty. Harold Applewhite took her into his little office.

"Miloria," he purred. "That was magnificent! Let me offer you a brandy to calm your nerves. I should be so delighted if you would come out with me to *Chez Gérard* this evening for dinner. I do so admire you, Miloria." And he gazed at her adoringly.

"Oh, Mr Applewhite, er – Harold," she cried. "How wonderful!"

Cowley Encounters
Penny Macleod

I'm looking for my son. I'm a middle class highly-educated woman with a standard of living to prove it. I live in a rambling house near Oxford, holidays abroad every year – you know the score. If you'd told me ten years ago that my life would come to this, I'd have laughed and said that only happened to dysfunctional families. But on this night of the winter solstice, I'm searching for my twenty-four year old son up and down the Cowley Road. He's renting a room in Temple Cowley, but the lease finishes tomorrow, he won't answer his phone, and I haven't heard from him for two weeks.

But he's twenty-four, you say. Surely he can look after himself? Well yes, up to a point. But let me tell you why I haven't cut the apron strings entirely. Milo does not yet understand how to be grown up; he doesn't want responsibility. When he dropped out of university and lolled around at home, friends gave me the usual well-meaning advice.

"Kick him out – then he'll have to get a job."

After six months, my husband said enough was enough, and Milo would indeed have to move out. He was right. If he hadn't had the courage to call time, Milo could well have been sitting at home on his thirtieth birthday, still not doing anything.

Oh, come *on*, you say. He would have got bored and pulled himself together long before that. Er, well, I'm not sure that he would. You see, Milo is capable of living an intense and meaningful life within his own head and on the internet. He is well-informed, has a good knowledge of films, and can hold a good conversation about the subtleties of US and British television comedy. He's intelligent and articulate. But although he has friends, they're a small, select bunch, and he never brings them home. And yet this is the boy who was in all the school teams, who laughed and joked, and had plenty of friends; who had starring parts in school plays, and taught himself the guitar.

The Eid lights sparkle and twinkle, suspended up above the Cowley Road, and I think back to the time when I was pregnant with Milo, and we lived in a Muslim country. There were many instances of intolerance there, but they are free here to practise their religion and celebrate the holiday at the end of Ramadan with the Cowley Road Eid lights. We could not hold Christian services in Saudi Arabia. If you wanted to buy a Christmas tree, you had to go into a secret storeroom at the back of the toy supermarket. Money changed hands there, not at the till; it was like buying an illicit substance. The illegal article then had to be carried out under a tarpaulin, and hidden in the car boot.

And yet what they have and we lack, is a strong sense of family. They are horrified at the way we dump our old people in homes, or make ghettoes for them in their sheltered housing. And when I go into Milo's favourite low-price grocery store to ask Mrs Patel when she last saw my son, she looks at me with pity. How on earth, she thinks, can it be possible that I haven't kept tabs on my son? To her, family is family; adulthood does not result in loss of contact at any point.

The pubs are next. I'm not quite sure why I'm checking them out – he's not much of a drinker. It's just the hope of a chance encounter in a public space that leads me onward. In one of them is a slot machine, on which a lad pulls and pushes buttons with manic intensity. Milo likes those slot machines; he's a risk-taker. I remember when he was about six years old, I looked out of a window and saw him crawling along the pergola above the patio, stalking the cat. Then his risks became more sophisticated – one of his near-expulsions from school involved selling downloaded DVDs in the playground.

In the plant shop I bump into my friend Karen, who is buying mistletoe. Karen is a white witch and tells me she is preparing to cast some splendid spells tonight. The magic is powerful at the solstices, and this is the time, says Karen, to achieve your dearest wish. Though of course, she adds, be careful what you wish for. A lightning bolt strikes.

"Karen, I haven't heard from Milo for two weeks and I'm desperate to find him. Could you work a spell for me?"

"Consider it sorted," says Karen.

I can see your disbelief as I tell you this. But what would you do in my position?

I know that Milo will do something good with his life. But it's as though he's enjoying the power game of making us all wait on tenterhooks, worrying to death that he might just screw up. He has had a succession of jobs way below his capabilities. He makes just enough to pay the rent most of the time, admittedly with the occasional loan from me. I have hope that he'll find his way, though. The last time I met him for lunch, he'd had two entrepreneurial ideas. The first was a mobile phone charging unit for use at music festivals – where teenagers always run out of battery so their parents can't contact them. The second was for software designed to help schoolchildren who found conventional learning methods didn't work for them. He told me that he had been that sort of child.

"They labelled me as disruptive," he told me, "but they just couldn't engage me. They talked and talked, but I wanted to see things happen, to be involved in activity and experience. Adults talking at me make me switch off and seek amusement elsewhere."

"I'd noticed," I said.

Call me kooky, but I feel an intuition coming on. I'm going to pop into the church hall. Until recently there was no way Milo would have been seen dead in a church hall. Then he met Mahmoud. Mahmoud is an engaging character who runs inter-faith gatherings here every Thursday, and I remember Milo talking about this chap. He's a Muslim cleric, and he invites people of different faiths to address his congregation; that's why his services are designated as 'gatherings' and can't be held in a mosque. Milo is clearly fascinated by Mahmoud.

Today is Thursday, so Mahmoud will be here. I'll slip in at the back. There's a wind getting up, blowing a couple of empty beer cans around my feet – now it's really gusting – I can barely open the door before it bangs shut. Christ, what's that? That branch of mistletoe appeared to drop from the roof. Then I notice that the hall is festooned with mistletoe. Mahmoud's group of people are sitting in a circle. They're enjoying themselves – the laughter reverberates round the Hall. Mahmoud is talking about the challenges of inter-faith marriages – and there is my son, sitting in the circle. He holds hands with a girl wearing a Moslem headscarf. Should I stay, or should I go? Slowly, he turns his head towards me, and smiles. It's as if he's been expecting me.

I smile back at my son; relief floods through me. Mahmoud sees me and asks if I'd like to join the circle. Milo stands up and greets me with a kiss.

"Mum, this is Leila, and we're going to get married."

I study my future daughter-in-law, and think how pretty she would look if her hair was set free to frame that face. I turn to my son:

"Milo, I'm so happy for you." And I am, because he is happy and sure of himself again. I invite them to come and have lunch with us at the weekend.

I must rush home and tell my husband what's happened. Then I'll call Karen and thank her. You wonder how the young couple will deal with the cultural gulf between them? So do I. But all I care about right now is that I've found my son again.

Oligarchs in Oxford
Yvonne Hands

A hotel in Oxford. The penthouse suite. The Garch family are sitting together in the most luxurious room in the hotel. GRANDPA GARCH, FATHER GARCH, and OLLIE, his son. OLLIE has a flawless English accent and is very English in his behaviour. FATHER GARCH is a crude Russian oligarch, with a heavy Russian accent. GRANDPA has a slight Russian accent overlaid with a very posh English accent.

FATHER GARCH   You want <u>what</u>?

OLLIE   To be a priest.

FATHER   *(in tones of total disbelief)*   A priest?

OLLIE   To serve God. To help people. To help the poor and needy.

FATHER *(screaming)*   Poor and needy! *(louder)* Poor and needy! I not kill about three hundred! Maim about two thousand and put fear of God into most of Russia to help poor and needy!

GRANDPA   And don't forget the Chechens.

FATHER *(coldly)*   I don't count Chechens as human beings.

GRANDPA *(fondly)*   Just like Stalin.

Father nods appreciatively.

GRANDPA *(chuckles, then turns serious)*   Ollie boy, you come from a great tradition. The Garchs help the poor and needy? Of course. We remove them to a better world.

FATHER   Enough of this. I buy you machine gun for birthday, Ollie. Now we show you how to use it.

Ollie ignores his father.

FATHER *(wheedling)*   Look Ollie, I do best for you. I send you to Eton, now to Oxford. Then the City. Everything to make you first-class shit. How you repay me? You want to serve God! What God do for you? What for me? You think I am one of richest men in world through God? Nancy boys for Church, not real men!

OLLIE (*very coldly*)   Nancy boys like Dietrich Bonhoeffer?

FATHER   Where stupid idea of Church come from?

OLLIE   Well actually, a friend of mine, an absolutely marvellous person.

FATHER (*sneering*)   A nancy boy.

OLLIE   A woman actually. A very dear friend.

GRANDPA (*chuckling*)   Ha, ha, a lady. I like ladies. I'm glad you have a lady at last. What is most noticeable feature of her?

He cups his hands in the air, suggesting big breasts.

OLLIE (*thinks for a minute*)   Well, she's black.

FATHER (*faintly*)   Black.

OLLIE   Yes. Very black actually. But the most inspiring and wonderful priest. I intend to marry her. She has, to my great surprise, accepted me.

GRANDPA   Black... Black... Marry... Black grandchildren.

Grandpa starts to scream, then bangs his head against the door, continuously. Father joins in, screaming and banging. There is a knock on the door. Ollie opens it.

HOTEL MANAGER   Is there a problem here?

GRANDPA (*screaming*)   Black, oh God, Black! <u>Black!</u>

HOTEL MANAGER (*icily*)   Yes, I am. As the ace of spades. Does that bother you? Shall I fetch the police and we can sort this out?

FATHER (*hastily*)   Nothing personal.

He pauses for a moment, thinking.

I have just told my father that his great friend, Conrad Black, is in prison, and he is beside himself with grief. Black is a great personal friend of his.

HOTEL MANAGER We all feel the loss. He was one of our best customers. We think fondly of the last time he came here. He left a tip!

He turns to Grandpa.

You didn't know Lord Black was in prison? The trial was in all the papers.

GRANDPA No, I've not been out of Russia for sixty years. I live in a very remote corner of Siberia. We hear nothing there.

HOTEL MANAGER If you'll pardon a personal remark – your English is remarkable. Almost perfect with an exquisite accent.

GRANDPA That is due to our great friends the Germans.

He leans forward in his chair.

Right at the beginning of the War, our War, I was taken prisoner by the Germans. The Germans behaved terribly to the Russian prisoners. One out of two died. But I had the great good fortune to be sent to a camp that was mainly for British officers. To cut a long story short, they protected me. All my comrades died. Every one. But the British officers hid me, and even passed me off as one of their own. They were great. As a result I learnt English – I had to, in order to survive as one of them. And of course their English was very upper class.

HOTEL MANAGER Ah, that's it. It reminds me of some of our members here.

GRANDPA As a matter of fact I have come over specially in my old age, to see if I can find some of them – and reward them. I wish to repay them. Especially one, who saved my life several times.

He smiles fondly, and says slowly:

Simon Bagshaw-Smythe.

HOTEL MANAGER (*amazed*)   But Lord Bagshaw-Smythe is a member here. As a matter of fact, he is here now. Terribly sad – really tragic – there is an auction tomorrow of his family home, Bagshaw Castle. His family has lived there for six hundred years. But now it has to go under the hammer.

GRANDPA   Could you find him?

HOTEL MANAGER   I'll go now.

GRANDPA   Jolly good show!

The Oligarchs' room, moments later. The Manager appears in the doorway with Lord Bagshaw-Smythe.

HOTEL MANAGER   His Lordship was just walking by and I managed to catch him.

His Lordship looks round the room, puzzled.

GRANDPA   Stalag IV.

His Lordship is startled. He goes up to Grandpa and peers at him. Grandpa looks back at him steadily.

LORD BAGSHAW-SMYTHE (*suddenly*) Ivan.

GRANDPA   Sixty years and you still know me.

LORD BAGSHAW-SMYTHE It's those eyes. They're different colours.

Grandpa suddenly becomes emotional, and clutches His Lordship's hands.

GRANDPA   Ah, Simon, I remember those days. You kept us poor Russian prisoners alive, sharing your rations with us.

LORD BAGSHAW-SMYTHE   Yes, the Germans treated the Russian prisoners very badly.

GRANDPA   God bless you.

LORD BAGSHAW-SMYTHE   I'm afraid he's not blessing me now. I'm here to auction off my whole estate. Been in my family for six hundred years. Nothing will be left. Also there's no one to inherit. My daughter is a widow, and has only two daughters herself.

Father Garch is suddenly interested.

FATHER   How old is your daughter?

LORD BAGSHAW-SMYTHE   She's thirty-eight. She was a late child for my wife and I. She is still rather beautiful.

FATHER   Does your daughter have big...

He cups his hands in the air.

HOTEL MANAGER (*butting in*)   Exceedingly!

FATHER (*excitedly*)   I will marry your daughter.

Lord Bagshaw-Smythe looks dubious.

FATHER (*sadly*)   Look, I have ten sons. All bastards, I never married. I can only get sons. I am very rich, I am still young, I am pretty. I have very big...

OLLIE (*aghast*)   Father!

LORD BAGSHAW-SMYTHE (*puffing*)   My dear chap.

GRANDPA   Don't show off.

LADY CAROLINE (Lord Bagshawe-Smythe's daughter) enters.

LADY CAROLINE   How big?

FATHER   Enormous!

Father Garch gets down on one knee.

Lady Caroline, will you marry me? I would like to be married and be English Lord. I give you sons and billions of roubles. Billions!

LADY CAROLINE   Granted. My room is upstairs.

FATHER   No, legit this time. We go church.

LADY CAROLINE   We have our very own church. We'll see the vicar now.

Father Garch and Lady Caroline exit, hand in hand.

LORD BAGSHAW-SMYTHE   We'll drink to that.

He pours a vodka from a bottle on a side table, and offers the glass to Grandpa.

GRANDPA   No, I only drink out of tooth mug from Stalag.

He reaches under his chair and brings out a battered tin mug with a huge swastika emblazoned on it.

LORD BAGSHAW-SMYTHE   My God, I do the same!

He produces a similar battered mug with a swastika.

LORD BAGSHAW-SMYTHE   As in the Camp…

They drink it down in one gulp, then raise their right arms in a Nazi salute.

LORD BAGSHAW-SMYTHE/GRANDPA (*simultaneously*)   Heil Hitler!

Arms entwined, they exit, laughing.

Loneliness
Val Watkins

The old man was drunk and high. It was one o'clock in the morning. Snow was falling as he swayed along New Inn Hall Street in Oxford, humming feebly. He tottered past the Ecco Shoe Shop and giggled as the snow bit into his cheeks and dropped on to his thin shoulders, which were covered by a useless torn overcoat. His shoes were no protection from the wetness underfoot and he started to breathe heavily as his steps became slower. He dragged his feet across George Street, got past the Odeon Cinema, and stumbled into Gloucester Green Square. He saw an empty doorway and lunged towards it with hard gulps of breath – shelter! But the snow was holding him back. As he pushed himself on a searing pain shot through his chest. He collapsed unconscious on to the ground.

"Oh no, it's him again. Didn't we pick him up a few weeks ago? Something's going to have to be done about him, I can tell you."

"He doesn't help himself, does he, and just look at the state of him. Ugh! And the pong and the filth!"

The paramedics in the ambulance watched as, in a daze, the old man struggled to sit up.

"All right, lie down. We're taking you to A&E. Just lie back now."

The old man moaned and flopped back.

"I'm not going in there again to be poked about by them doctors."

"Well, you should take more care of yourself then, shouldn't you!"

Strong hands gripped the stretcher as he was lifted out of the ambulance and into A&E at The John Radcliffe. Neon lights blazed through his head. A disdainful nurse tore off his threadbare clothes and put them into a black bin bag. He was taken to the shower, made to sit on a stool and given a vigorous wash. The nurse helped him into a hospital gown and he was deposited on to a bed and covered with blankets.

"Well, what is your name?" The nurse had a form on a clipboard.

"Fred Jackson."

"Address?"

"No fixed abode."

"Age?"

"78."

The nurse took his temperature and blood pressure.

"You're in a bad way, Fred. What have you been doing to yourself? Lie here and wait. The doctor will be round to see you later."

The doctor finished his examination and stood back to look at the old man.

"Well, Fred, you have certainly made a mess of yourself. Too much alcohol, but worse still, too much cocaine. Your angina can't cope with all this. Your life-style doesn't help. Homeless, mixing with drug addicts. We're going to get on to Social Services and see what they can suggest. But you've got to help yourself. You can't live like this any longer. This is the third time in two months you've ended up here. Another episode like this and you'll have a serious heart attack. Have you no family, wife, children, siblings?"

"Nah, just me. I did love a girl once, but 'er family didn't approve. Y' know the sort of thing. Always bin a wanderer, me, picking up jobs here and there. Fairgrounds, odd-jobbing, farm work, seasonal stuff. Later on living rough, wandering the country, never settling like. Couldn't get anything these last few years. Been sleeping in doorways down London, came here thinking it'd be better. But it isn't."

Fred fell back on to his pillows, his breath coming in gasps.

"We're sending you to the cardiology ward. Put an oxygen mask on him, nurse. We've more tests to do yet, Fred. You may have to stay in over Christmas."

Fred woke up from a deep sleep feeling more refreshed than he had for a long time. Curtains were drawn round his bed and he breathed easily through the oxygen mask. He could hear bustling by the next bed. Two nurses were making it up. One of them said,

"They're bringing him up from A&E now, poor lad. Found unconscious in his room. Oxford student."

"Right, here we are young fella. Let's just lift you on to the bed. Steady now, you just relax. Right, there we are."

The sound of curtains being drawn round the bed. A nurse talking to the new patient. Fred could not keep his eyes open and drifted off to sleep again.

Fred opened his eyes wearily. He could hear a doctor speaking to the patient in the next bed.

"You have been abusing your body, drinking heavily and using cocaine at these student drugs parties. You're having bouts of breathlessness because you have developed an irregular heartbeat. You must clean up your lifestyle and get proper exercise every day or you will damage your heart irrevocably. You are far too young to be in this state. We are going to perform a minor operation to get your heart beating regularly. Hopefully you'll be ready after a few days' rest."

The next time Fred woke up he heard a tea trolley rattling in the distance. He watched a nurse draw back the curtains round his neighbour. Fred saw a young man of about twenty, pale and sickly, lying on the bed. The tea trolley rattled nearer. A lady spoke to Fred.

"Tea, coffee, fruit drink, water?"

"Ooh, a nice cup o' tea, please."

"Biscuits?"

"Yes, please."

"And you, young man?"

"Nothing." He turned over and burrowed into his pillows.

The next morning, Fred was woken at six-thirty by the trolley girl again.

"Cereal, fruit, boiled egg? Cup of tea? Fruit juice?"

"Yeah," said Fred.

"No," said his neighbour.

"Y'ought to eat, keep yer strength up," said Fred.

"Leave me alone."

"It's for your own good, son."

"Look, I'm not your son, Grandad, and when I want your advice I'll ask for it."

More tests followed for Fred and the young man. They were told that they would have to stay in the ward until after Christmas. Both were visited by Social Services who were looking into aftercare for them and accommodation for Fred. The young man's parents lived in Edinburgh. They had flown down to see him and when they went back home they phoned every day. Fred had no one.

'Grandad' regaled 'Son' with some stories of his lively past to cheer him up.

"There was the time when me and my mate Joe got some work on a farm for a day. Plantin' cabbages, it were. So we started – it took us all day. We went to the farmer to get our money and he nearly exploded! 'You've planted them the wrong way up!' he shouted. 'No pay for you two!' "

"Another time we got a fortnight strawberry picking and kept eating t' fruit as we went along. We got paid very well all right but spent t' first night in th' hostel with the trots! We didn't eat any more strawberries for the rest o' the time I can tell ye!"

It was good to see 'Son' laughing and it cheered Fred up no end to have his tales appreciated.

"Times weren't always funny, though. Many's the time we've been chased by t' police for nicking cans o' beer. I went to Manchester hoping things would be better there. I got in with a rough crowd who were dossing down in empty warehouses and condemned houses. Living rough and getting hold o' drugs by any means they could. Me, weak so-and-so that I was, just went along with them and got hooked on cannabis, then harder stuff and then cocaine. Stuck with t' same lot, hadn't the will to break away from them. Then I would move as folk died or ended up in prison. It were like that wherever I went. Always fell in with t' wrong lot. I've bin in London for many years. Came to Oxford a couple o' years ago."

Next day 'Son' had some visitors, three students from the university. They chatted to 'Son' and Fred saw them give him a brown paper bag.

"What do you want to bring me these grapes for?" said 'Son' to his mates.

"To eat, you idiot!"

They laughed and giggled. Fred was pleased to see his neighbour livening up a bit. The friends visited a few more times before Christmas. They went home after that to their families.

A man from the Oxford Night Shelter came to see Fred. He told him he could use the emergency accommodation at O'Hanlon House when he came out of hospital. Fred thought it sounded as though he would have to behave himself. He wasn't sure if he could.

It was Christmas Eve.

"How're you feeling today then, Son? You're looking a bit brighter. Ye've been eating better. Food's not too bad in 'ere."

"No, but I'd rather be at home so I could go out partying with my mates."

"What, and get into the state you were in when you first came in here?"

"What about you Grandad? You're hardly in top-notch condition!"

"No, I'm not. Take warning from me and t' mess I'm in. I've abused me body and lived rough and now I've nowhere to go and nobody to care about what happens to me."

The young man looked at him.

"Social Services'll take care of you. There's a Night Shelter in O'Hanlon House and you can opt for the Resettlement Unit there and they'll help you with all your problems. You would be supported by their Link Workers. You'd have to behave yourself though and not drink or do drugs. They'll get you sorted. I've been researching it all for my degree. I'm supposed to be doing some voluntary work and learning experience there after Christmas. That's if I'm fit enough.

"There's a place in Yarnton, The Ley Community, as well, for young people like me. I've heard it's very tough there. Don't think I could hack it though, I need my fixes."

Fred spluttered and nearly choked, "Are you mad? Learn your lesson! You've had a narrow escape. Don't even think about fixes. When's your op, Son?"

"Day after Boxing Day, Grandad. Then I can go back home, or to my room in College."

It was one of the best Christmas dinners Fred had ever eaten. He sat up in bed with his red paper hat nearly down over his eyes and savoured his turkey and Christmas pudding.

"Well, Son, that was delicious. I feel really full after that lot!"

"Yeah, Grandad. It was OK. I'd rather be at home though. Then I could be off with my mates tonight. It's pretty boring in here."

"Well, thanks for nothing."

"Didn't mean you. I'd have gone round the bend if I hadn't had you and your stories to listen to, Grandad. You've kept me sane."

The day of the operation arrived. 'Son' was prepared and given his premeds.

"You'll be fine, Son, I'll have one of me tales ready for ye when ye come back."

'Son' waved a limp hand in his direction. "Bye, Grandad, see you soon."

Then he was wheeled away down the ward. Fred read his paper and then settled down for a little nap.

He slept for a long time. He woke up feeling dizzy and disoriented. He looked across at 'Son's' bed. He stared. It had been stripped completely and a nurse was washing the rubber mattress with disinfectant.

"Eeh, you've not moved him have you? We're good mates!"

The nurse looked at him strangely.

"I'm sorry, Fred. The young chap had a heart attack during the operation. There was nothing anybody could do. He's dead."

Fred was stunned.

"Bu-but he was doing well!"

"I'm afraid not, Fred. His so-called friends brought him cocaine hidden in with his grapes. We found some in his cupboard. He must have been dosing himself in the toilets. His heart couldn't take it."

Fred lay very still. The sight of the empty bed was unbearable. He could hear 'Son's' voice telling him about Oxford's help for homeless people. He would ring them tomorrow. It was the least he could do for 'Son'.

The X-mas Factor
Birte Milne

"That's our Molly," the man next to him whispered proudly. "Better than any of them hopefuls on 'X Factor', that's for sure."

Simon smiled back and nodded.

"Oh, yes, she's got real talent."

Most of her talent was in the amount of bare flesh this Molly was exposing and the way she kept flicking her long, false eyelashes in the direction of the judges. The notes coming from the heavily made-up mouth certainly gave him no cause for concern.

Simon felt quietly confident and suitably nervous. A few nerves were good to get the adrenaline going and help you 'keep your eye on the ball'. Too many and it affected the voice and breathing. If he could stay like this until it was his turn, he would have nothing to worry about. From what he'd seen during that afternoon's rehearsals, this night would be his for sure.

Molly finished her Mariah Carey impression of 'All I Want for Christmas is You', much to the embarrassed relief of the audience. The man next to him, obviously the proud father, jumped to his feet clapping wildly and shouting, "Bravo! Bravo!" Polite applause echoed from the rest of the hall. Molly looked down towards her supporters' group and attempted to curtsey within the confines of her tight leather mini skirt.

The presenter walked onto the stage and physically guided Molly off backstage.

"Thank you to our first contestant, Molly Partridge, and her wonderful Mariah Carey song," he said into the microphone. "If this first song is anything to go by, I can see this is going to be a very interesting evening."

And very long, Simon thought.

Simon was listed twelfth on the programme and there were twenty-one acts in total. He wasn't on until after the break, so at least he would have a chance to go outside for some fresh air and get his mind in focus. He looked around the hall stuffed with the familiar faces of the whole neighbourhood. This was definitely a special Saturday night out for most of them. Usually, not a lot of interest happened around Quarry so every Tom, Dick and Harry and his Granny had turned up tonight to support their favourite act.

Simon caught a glimpse of his friend Danny. Danny saw him looking and gave an encouraging thumbs-up. This had been Danny's idea right from the beginning when they saw the poster displayed outside the Community Center.

X Factor Auditions

Saturday 1st December

The winner will perform on 23rd December at the Annual Christmas Concert in Oxford Town Hall

---

"This is your chance! This is how you make Sophie fall head over heels," Danny had shouted, brimming with excitement.

Simon hadn't been that sure to begin with. The way he felt about Sophie, and the way she made him feel, was a sore point between them. Simon wished he could be as direct and confident as his friend where women were concerned. Mostly he was fine because he wasn't interested in them, but with Sophie it was just impossible. She ticked all the boxes for his dream woman, and touched spots he'd forgotten existed just by waving to him out of her classroom window.

In the end Danny had had to pull out all the stops to convince him.

"Simon, let's face it. She doesn't know you exist and you two are meant for each other. She will be organising this. She may even be one of the judges. This is just perfect."

"No way. I just couldn't. They'll all think I'm a joke and boo me off stage."

Simon's talent and love for singing had been a big secret right until Danny had caught him, back in the summer, belting out 'Nessun Dorma', Pavarotti style, while he was trimming the hedge in Mrs Blackburn's Shotover garden. Danny's reaction had been unexpected and one of complete admiration.

"Wow," he'd said, very quietly. "That sent shivers down my spine. How did you ever learn to sing like that Simon, without me, your best mate, having a bloody clue that you could?"

Simon's embarrassment had turned to utter relief and immense pride.

"I've never told anyone before. Dad and the boys would most likely throw me out if they knew. You should hear their comments when we watch 'X Factor' and it's the guys' turn. Singing's for poofs."

"But how did you find out you could? Who taught you?"

"Nobody. I've always been singing, when I was sure no one could hear me. And working outdoors and in big gardens, it's the perfect place to have a secret like this."

With the relief at finally being able to share his secret the words had come stumbling out, with hardly any room to breathe. The faint memories of his mother always singing when he was little. His mother's things packed away in the attic after her death with the music scores and recordings. His den in the bottom shed, where he could practise and learn new songs and his home-made alarm system with strings and bells to warn him if his dad or brothers came near.

Danny had listened silently, unable to get a word in, even if he'd wanted to. He had been completely lost for words. When Simon had finally got everything off his chest, Danny had given him a manly slap on the back and cleared his throat repeatedly, before he was ready to speak.

"I think we should change our company logo from 'PRUNING 4 U' to 'TUNING 4 U'. That is, if you could teach me to sing too."

"I'm not quite ready to let the rest of the world know yet," Simon had laughed, "so let's stick to pruning for now."

Their friendship had become even stronger, with the sharing of Simon's secret and the open admiration and encouragement Danny showed him. Simon had gradually become more relaxed about having another human listening instead of just the usual birds, squirrels and occasional hedgehog. He had even ventured to sing when he risked being heard by the owners of the gardens they were working in. The surprised glances had given him the confidence to attempt even more challenging songs.

Simon was brought back to the stage in the Community Centre, when the presenter announced the last act before the break.

"Act eleven. The Barbershop Quartet, 'Short Back and Sides', will now be singing 'Winter Wonderland'." They got tremendous applause.

As the break was announced, Simon made his way to the exit where he had arranged to meet Danny. He nearly collided with Sophie in the doorway.

"Hello Sophie. Great turnout. Wonderful talent," was all he could utter.

Why did she make him feel like this, when he could chatter away to any other girl he met on a Saturday night at The Six Bells? When Sophie talked to him, during his weekly visits to cut the grass in the school playing fields; the way she made him feel now: all tight chested and sweaty palmed; it was just so embarrassing. She was the head teacher at the school, but that was no reason for him to feel like a ten-year-old schoolboy. She was always so sweet to him and didn't let on if she had any idea how awkward he felt.

"You're next, after the break," she said with a big smile. "I hear you caused quite a stir at this afternoon's rehearsals."

He could only nod.

"Good luck, Simon," she added quietly, reaching up to plant a kiss on his cheek, then she squeezed his arm as she walked past him out into the foyer.

Danny was waiting for him outside the front door, chewing nervously on a cigarette end.

"Where've you been? We're losing time."

Simon was touching the wet on his cheek where Sophie had kissed him, looking back at Danny slightly dazed.

"What's the matter, Simon? Are you OK?"

"OK? Yes, I think so."

Danny looked puzzled. The two went backstage to prepare. Twenty minutes later Danny left Simon to take his seat in the hall. Simon could hardly breathe, and felt his heart beating so loudly he only hoped it wouldn't be louder than his voice.

The lights were dimmed and only the white from Danny's knuckles clutching the armrests showed in the dark.

"Go for it, Simon," Danny whispered. "Give it to them!"

"Now for our first act after the interval. As number twelve we have Simon Turner singing 'You Raise Me Up'. Are you ready Simon?"

The presenter looked towards Simon, still standing in the wings. Simon took a deep breath and nodded. He walked quickly onto the stage towards the microphone, almost blinded by the strong spotlights. He couldn't make out any of the faces in the darkness below him, but sensed the closeness of the awaiting audience. A strange calmness of anonymity came over him. He was here all alone in the power of the spotlights, blinding the world around him.

The musical intro began and soon he was lost to the words and notes flowing effortlessly from his lips. He sang as he'd never sung before.

Much too quickly, it was all over and for a moment he thought he was still all alone. There was what seemed like an eternity of complete silence. Then the hall erupted in a roar of applause and cheering, taking Simon completely aback. He made an awkward bow and hurried off stage as quickly as his shaking legs could take him. He needed to get out, breathe the fresh air.

"Did you see her face? I've never seen anyone look so surprised. And the way her eyes were welling up. You sure made her see what you're made of." Danny was speaking out of breath, having dashed outside trying to catch up with Simon.

"I didn't mean to make her cry," Simon answered, sadly.

"Oh no, she looked more like – full of emotion – you know. Bursting with affection."

Danny was full of excitement. Simon just felt tired and more confused than ever.

"What now?" he said quietly.

"Don't worry mate, I'm sure you'll grow to like being famous."

The two of them walked back into the hall and sat down quietly at the back, just in time to hear the presenter thanking act twenty-one, a full faced, grey-haired pensioner, for her rendition of 'We'll meet again'.

"And now, we have a late, unexpected entry, which is not in the programme," the presenter continued. "Act number twenty-two, Craig Entwistle, who decided to enter this afternoon, when he delivered the food for our late supper, which we'll all enjoy while your votes are counted and our judges make their deliberations. Please welcome Craig, who will not only be filling your stomachs this evening, but also your ears, singing 'When a Child is Born'."

Simon sat upright in his seat and watched silently. When Craig hit his first note, Simon knew he was in trouble.

"Nothing's for sure yet," Danny said.

"Oh, spare me the waffle," Simon whispered back. "I know when I'm beaten." Simon slid quietly out of his seat and left the hall.

The event made the headlines in the Oxford Mail the following Monday.

**TALENT CONTEST WITH
UNEXPECTED OUTCOME**

For the people of
Headington, this year's
X-mas Factor auditions
had a very unhappy
ending, for more than the
unlucky contestants. More
than fifty people present
at the event, including
all the judges, developed
acute food poisoning
during the late supper,
and voting had to be
abandoned.

Health Officials suspect
contaminated prawns
supplied by 'Entwistle
Catering' to be the
culprit and are starting
a full investigation.

Headington will have to
wait another year to be
represented at Oxford's
Annual Christmas Concert
in the Town Hall.

The following Saturday Simon went to meet Danny at The Six Bells for their usual night out. He was late, having nearly chickened out at the last moment. He wasn't sure that he was ready to face being seen in public yet after his fiasco of a coming-out performance on stage. In the end it was a matter of choosing the lesser of two evils, and going to The Six Bells won over spending an evening in being quizzed by Dad and the boys, while having to watch 'Match of the Day'.

The pub seemed unusually empty for a Saturday night. The sharp frost and threat of snow is keeping everyone else at home tonight,

Simon thought. What a relief. He looked around for Danny and, somewhat surprised at not finding him in their usual corner, Simon ventured into the back part of the pub. The sight that met him there made him hesitate for a moment, unsure whether to turn around and just leg it. The room was filled to the brim with people, balloons, streamers and banners displaying his name. And there at the back he saw Danny's gleaming face greeting him with a loud cheer which was echoed from around the room. Simon felt himself being pushed forward towards the middle of the room and hands clapping his shoulders left and right as he passed through the crowd.

"Well done, Mate!"

"Stole the show, you did!"

"Won it hands down!"

"Definitely our X-mas Factor winner!"

Simon's embarrassment and shyness was slowly evaporating as he saw the sincerity with which all these people were showering their praise. Perhaps his performance hadn't been such a fiasco after all.

And then he saw her sitting there, half hidden behind Danny's sturdy figure. He watched as she pushed her chair back before standing up and then coming slowly towards him. Everything else in the room ceased to matter.

"Damn that Craig Entwistle and his bloody prawns," she said. "I may be biased, but you were the only X-mas Factor winner, as far as I could see."

Before Simon had the chance to reply, he felt Sophie's arms pull him towards her and as their lips met he knew he'd just won the best prize he could ever have wanted.

And for the second time within a week his performance made the room erupt in a roar of applause, cheering and calls for an encore.

The Scoop
Graham Bird

I pulled into the car park of Grayson Enterprises just after 5 o'clock. The January frost gave the world a calmness that Bessie did her best to shatter as she slid to a halt in the far corner space, facing the reception entrance.

Dave is always telling me that Bessie will let me down one day but she hasn't done yet. I wanted a 2CV ever since my French teacher gave me a lift to school one day. I had to push the empty *Gitanes* packets and crisp bags onto the floor as I got in. The smell was exhilarating and romantic. He was Mr Laupetre, or *Monsieur Laupêtre* as we had to call him. We lived in the same street, and yes, all my friends were very jealous. Fifteen years later, there I was, driving one, and not speaking a word of French.

The car park was dotted with a few overnight cars, each covered in a glistening white sheet making them eerily similar. I turned off Bessie's lights and settled down into the seat, wrapping my scarf tighter, and lit up my second of the day.

"Now then, Mr Grayson. It's show-time." I turned on my camera.

Five minutes later, a Jaguar drove slowly through the car park entrance and stopped right in front of the main office doors. The passenger leaned over and kissed the driver, a lingering early morning kiss from a lover. I started to think about headlines as I pressed the shutter: 'Grayson grabs his girl'. His fingers gently stroked the driver's long blonde hair as he kissed her, then Grayson got out of the car and hurried into the building, not looking back. I ducked over to the passenger seat, hiding from the glare of the headlights as the car moved past, then I pulled Bessie's starter. She coughed in just the same way as I do after each drag, and jumped into life. We merged into the traffic on the London Road, three cars behind the Jag and followed it all the way to its home just off the Iffley Road, then I headed toward the office. It was still only 5:45am but I knew the newsroom would be busy.

"So, this Grayson, so he's having an affair. So what?" Meet my editor, Doug Lowe. He stared down at the prints of thirty snaps.

"Well, he's married with three children, and he's Chief Executive of Grayson Enterprises," I said.

"So we ruin his life. Great. Hundreds of people have affairs, Linda. Is that it?"

"No. That's not it. You see the blonde?"

Doug squinted at the close-up of the woman's face through the windscreen. "I can hardly make it out. Does it matter who she is?"

"Look. I know you've seen hundreds of these indiscretions in your twenty years at the Gazette." I couldn't resist a tiny note of sarcasm in my review of Doug's career. I loved him when he was tetchy.

"Don't get lippy, Miss White. I need more than a blurry blonde to make this a story."

"How about if I tell you this is none other than Janice Jones, better known as Janey Jones, a well known Oxford party girl. A glamorous heiress. Does that start to sound better?"

"Still no."

"Oh, and there's one other small point to mention." I enjoyed the tension. "Janey Jones is daughter of Ron Jones, the Chairman and major shareholder of Onmark Marketing, the main competitor of Grayson Enterprises. Now, there's some pillow talk potential." I sat back.

Doug's face cracked. "Lindy. Now that, my girl, that is a story."

I smiled back. Doug was the only person I allowed to call me Lindy.

I didn't get back to the flat until past midnight and Dave was already asleep. I stripped in the dark and slid into bed beside him and lay back, wide awake. It had been a late night getting the layout finished, just making the deadline after endless minor adjustments to appease Doug.

When the daylight pushed its way through the curtain, I thought I'd been awake all night, but Dave was gone and there was the aroma of coffee coming from the kitchen where the radio was playing 'New Kids on the Block' at full blast. Dave was singing.

I ran down to the front door and picked up the morning papers. Ever since college, I'd spoiled myself with paper deliveries. All the tabloids and locals – it's necessary for the job, I justified.

I straightened out the Oxford Gazette onto the kitchen table. 'Grayson caught'. It was the simple headline that Doug had chosen.

Dave stood behind me and wrapped his arms round, kissing me on my neck just below my ear. "Is that Charles Grayson? Grayson Enterprises?" I leaned back into his warmth and shut my eyes.

"Indeed it is, and that is my first front page. Woo-hoo. At least there haven't been any overnight world catastrophes to spoil the moment this time. When I had that scoop about The Bodleian along came a horrendous road crash on the A34. You remember."

Meet Dave, my steady boyfriend of five months now. The sensible one in a regular job, not like the crazy escapades of my early twenties, but mysterious enough to be interesting. I'm going to be thirty this year. Time to get serious.

"Aha." Dave sat back and bit at his toast as he carefully read every word and studied the photo. Then he turned to the exposé on pages four and five, still not speaking. An irritating habit.

"Wow," he said. "What can I say? Hard to believe, that's for sure. Quite the story."

"Well, it's clear isn't it? It's all about the corruption."

"And the girl? How did she take it, when she knew she'd been snapped?"

"Oh, I don't know. It's not about her. It's Grayson we have."

Dave seemed to hesitate.

"What, what's wrong?" I said.

"Nothing, nothing. Great story darling. Well done. I have to dash. Meeting at 8:30."

Dave kissed me on the cheek and grabbed his briefcase as he shut the front door, just as the phone rang.

"Yes, yes, thanks Doug. Thanks so much. It looks great. I'll be in soon."

"No, don't come in Lindy. Go and see Janey Jones – wait outside her house. See who turns up."

I smiled at my face in the mirror. Lindy has done a good job.
Bessie purred as I drove down the Cowley Road. There was a pride in her. I pulled up behind a dark blue Escort halfway down the street from Janey's house, and sat back to wait. The smoke filled Bessie like a Victorian smog. I wiped the camera lens.

There were a couple of reporters hanging around at the end of the street that I recognised from an Oxford Press Association party. I pushed myself further down in the seat, getting used to the surveillance jobs now.

After my first cup of coffee from the flask, Grayson's Jag pulled into the street and stopped directly outside the house. Grayson looked dishevelled as he got out and knocked at the door. Was he really that scruffy, or just casual instead of suited? I couldn't be sure. Perhaps he'd been up all night. I took a few pictures as the door opened and he went in.

After five minutes a second car stopped outside, a Mercedes, and an older, smarter gentleman got out. Ron Jones.

I started to scribble some notes and timings, wishing I could hear the exchanges inside. I could imagine. They would be working out various excuses, preparing a statement for the press. Should I knock? I hesitated and Charles Grayson came out of the house and drove away quickly, then Ron Jones left too. I snapped away but regretted missing the moment, and decided that I could at least present myself to Janey Jones. It was worth the risk.

I brushed out my hair and fixed my makeup in Bessie's mirror, then opened the door intending to step onto the pavement. As I did, I froze. Was that Dave? In that car? It is Dave. What's he doing here?

I sank back into the seat, wishing Bessie to be invisible but didn't need to worry. Dave strode quickly to Janey's front door without glancing anywhere near my direction. I watched, not believing. Does he know Janey? Surely not. My stomach flipped.

I guess my training kicked in. All those lectures on the art of journalism and how you had to stay detached. This wasn't my boyfriend, my Mr Sure-But-Steady future. This was a potential follow-up. I focussed the zoom and snapped my camera as the door opened and Dave was greeted with a hug before walking into the house. She even had the cheek to look up and down the street like she was checking for onlookers as she ushered him in.

Bessie grumbled all the way back to the office and I flounced into Doug's office with my latest scoop.

"Sit down, calm yourself Lindy." Doug's smile was reassuring, and he put a comforting hand on my shoulder.

"He's a bastard. Why didn't he tell me he knew her? There's only one reason, that's for sure."

"Look, forget him now. So he's lying. So what? All us men do."

"Not him, not Dave. That's the point."

Doug sighed and I could see the sympathy drain from his eyes. "What's the storyline, Miss White?"

"Well, I guess it's that this Janey Jones puts it about a bit. Shares the secrets with all sorts, and shares whatever else I guess. Slut."

"Lindy. Professional journalism please."

We worked on the story together and reviewed the photos I'd taken of Dave and Janey. Doug was encouraging and patient, none of his usual gruffness. I was pleased. Another front page loomed and two in a row would boost my career a hundredfold. I didn't want to go home, that's for sure. Once we'd finished and met the 10pm deadline, Doug suggested a beer.

"Just a quick one, to mark the next step in your career. And... I guess, with this story, your impending single status. Sorry Lindy."

It hadn't really hit me before but Doug was right. The bastard. Who needs him anyway? I sighed.

The alarm woke me. No Dave in bed. No sounds. I slipped on my gown and crept downstairs. He must have left already. I switched on the kitchen light and put on the kettle. When I turned to the table, I noticed the paper, laying flat, front page up.

'Janey does it again' headlined across the top in 48 font. Another one of Doug's. Underneath the photo of her hugging Dave on the doorstep. I sat and read the entire article once more. I smiled, at least I got the bastard.

Beside the paper was a folded note. I opened it.

Dear Linda,

Well, it's clear your career comes first then. Good luck with that. I hope you get a long way on it. As far from here as possible. I'm sure you'll be perfect for the daily tabloids, you're ready for them. And you'll fly high on a photo of me hugging my sister. Give my regards to Doug. Oh well, it was fun for a while. I'll pick up my stuff at the weekend.

Bye, Dave x

I screwed up the note and threw it at the mirror. Bastard.

A Fairy Story
Jenny Burrage

I know you but do you know me?
I'm the fairy on your Christmas tree!
I lead a horrid life all year
On January 12th I disappear.

Up to my box I have to go
Why is it you treat me so?
In that box it's cold and dark
Not a chink of light, not a tiny spark.

The prickly tinsel scratches my skin
The baubles are lumpy and squash me in
I'm not an ordinary fairy you know
I've got real naughty bits above and below!

Your children handle me oh so rough
I'm delicate you see, not tough
Last year the dog chewed a piece off my arm
You just don't care if I come to harm.

And so I've decided to moan today
I won't go on strike, that's not my way
Oh no, I've got another plan
Yes, try and stop me if you can.

Do you wonder why everyone's staring at me
As I strut my stuff at the top of the tree?
Well you might be surprised or maybe get shocks
I've left my knickers upstairs in the box!

The Annunciation
Julie Adams

Mary looked at the man standing before her. His white garments shone and there was bright light all around him. Her knees bent. Overcome with emotion, she started to sing.

"My soul doth magnify the Lord
And my spirit doth rejoice in God my saviour
For he hath regarded the lowliness of his handmaiden."

She felt the exact moment when the divine spark of new life entered her.'

The consultant stripped off his gloves and threw them in the clinical waste bin.

"I've never had one as out of it as that," he said. "Singing all the way through. 'The Messiah' or something."

"Just overdid it with the Rescue Remedy, I think," said the nurse. "Usually they listen to their iPods to help them relax."

"If she can't cope with the embryo transfer, how will she manage labour and delivery?" He pushed the taps off with his elbows. "But that, thankfully, is Obstetrics' problem."

"We just get 'em pregnant," agreed the nurse.

"Why has she come all the way to Oxford? Don't they have any sperm donors in Galashiels or Galloway or wherever it is they live?"

"I think her cousin Liz recommended us. She did IVF with us a while ago and she's six months pregnant now." The nurse stapled the photos from the scan into the patient's folder. "It's a little boy and her husband told me they're going to call him John." Zechariah

"Oh yes, I remember the husband; Zack or something. Didn't say much," said the doctor. He nodded at the door to the adjacent scan room. "We'll leave her with her acupuncturist for the moment."

"Yes, Dr Gabriel. Then I'll go and get her partner, Joseph, from the waiting room."

John born 26 June

The Christmas Gift
Neil Hancox

An ordinary weekday in the routine of life. The post landed with a gentle thud on the carpet. The woman walked down the hallway, picked up the mail and returned to the kitchen. She discarded charity appeals and adverts for pizza houses and takeaway curry parlours. The remaining envelope was hand-addressed to Mrs E J Dillaney.

She studied the first line of the address. The initials E.J. stood for Evangeline Jasmine, abbreviated to Evie. She could blame her parents for the choice of Christian names. The surname was her responsibility. James Dillaney had been faintly exotic, attractive and available. Only later did a combination of drinking and the occasional infidelity appear. That was over twenty-five years ago. She returned to the envelope. It must be an early Christmas card. Was the writing familiar? The postmark was obscured. No clue there. While Alfie, her black cat and companion, watched, she opened the envelope and extracted a picture of a cheery Santa sipping champagne in the company of an inebriated reindeer. Best wishes from…, a passing acquaintance.

Evie stood the card up on a corner of her kitchen table. Christmas was overrated, especially when it began too early. She played with a piece of toast and marmalade, while she tried to rid her memory of the late Mr Dillaney. It had not been her fault, though she had given him a bottle of fine malt whisky for his birthday. Neither were the stairs in their house highly polished, despite the gossip.

Why would two initials on an envelope trigger an avalanche of memories? She looked at Alfie. "No one could prove anything," she told him. "Even if there were anything to be proved," she added hurriedly. The cat was unmoved.

The ashes of the late Mr Dillaney had been consigned to the winds of Otmoor. In happier times the lovers had wandered across that wild place. After her husband's funeral Evie had felt a mixture of guilt and relief. She imagined the act of scattering ashes as one of reconciliation. Eventually forgetfulness had come, as her friends had said it would, and her life had continued – if she admitted it, pleasantly and predictably.

The telephone interrupted.

"Hello. Yes Amanda. No, I hadn't forgotten, Amanda. Goodbye."

Amanda was a worthy, plodding girl. Her imagination was limited and her vocal chords severely strained due to an almost perpetual cold.

Evie selected a padded ski jacket to protect against Oxford's special contribution to the cheer of Christmas: a penetrating wind flecked with spots of drizzle. She added a touch of lipstick and then completed her insulation with a fur hat, imitation of course, and similar gloves. The clothes made her modest figure plump but cosy. She wished that her years were more modest. Unfortunately it was becoming difficult to deceive herself. The bus pass was approaching.

Her preparations were complete. She picked up her small case and set out to walk from a living Jericho terrace house to an apartment in a decaying North Oxford mansion.

Half an hour later glowing, but slightly out of breath, Evie arrived. She noted that the number of stagnant cars in the driveway was unchanged since her last visit. Several dishevelled bicycles had also appeared among the ever-present weeds.

The bell was below the corroded brass panel that had once brightly announced 'Dr D Petters'. Evie pushed it hard. She heard the shuffling steps. The door opened to frame an aged retainer of somewhat indeterminate sex.

"Hello, it's you," the voice said. "Come in. He's waiting for you. Usual room at the back."

Evie nodded her thanks. She peeled off her jacket, dropped it onto a waiting chair and walked down the tiled passageway. She paused outside the door marked 'Dr Petters', knocked and waited for the indistinct, "Come," indicative she always thought of ill-fitting teeth and weary tonsils.

The man was sitting in a swivel chair beside a large desk. On its stained leatherette top there was a telephone, a pad of lined paper and two pens. Sharp brown eyes peered at her out of a shrivelled face. The trademark stethoscope was draped around the neck.

"And what's the problem, Mrs Dillaney?" a now rather more distinct voice enquired. Without waiting for a response, it added, "You look well to me, Mrs Dillaney. I suggest we keep you on your usual medication and you come back in a fortnight."

He smiled at her and she noticed that the skin on the hands was taut and yellowing. The first part of the charade was completed.

"You will," the doctor said, "take coffee with me."

An order, not a question. On cue a tray appeared with a pot of coffee, two cups, a jug of milk and some biscuits. Evie poured the coffee and selected a biscuit. The doctor smiled at her as she pushed his cup across the desktop towards him.

"I always enjoy my morning's refreshment," he said, sipping his drink.

When he had finished he rolled up his sleeve to expose his upper arm, Evie applied a dab of alcohol, administered the contents of the syringe and followed up with a plaster.

"My helping of instant sanity," he remarked. "That should keep the voices quiet."

The visit was over. The medication would last for a fortnight. As Evie was about to go he touched her hand and looked at her. She felt uncomfortable.

"I know your secret," he whispered, "but it will be safe with me. I shall take it to the grave."

He reached into a drawer and removed a small silver box which he handed to her. "That is a Christmas present for you."

Evie was surprised and confused. She blushed. She had known the doctor for over thirty years. In that time he had never touched her, other than professionally, and never given her a present.

"Thank you so much," she said.

It was a half-mile walk towards the centre of Oxford, to the office of 'In-House Medical Care'. Evie was puzzled. She had carried out her regular visits to the doctor for nearly five years now. Patient and carer both knew that the other knew, but it kept the patient in his own home and paid the carer well. Why had the old man suddenly chosen to speak of a secret? Anyway if it had been a secret it should have been theirs, not hers.

As she avoided the flow of early Christmas shoppers crowding the pavements, Evie wondered who would look after her one day. Alfie was already well into cat dotage and her relatives were distant and uninterested. Her modest pension and savings would not last long if she became ill. Perhaps she should have re-married, raised a family, though producing children to look after you later on in your life struck her as a selfish act.

The headquarters of her employer was in another North Oxford mansion. This time decay had been banished with a manicured drive and flowerbeds, and inside, pastel colours, oak panels and a touch of stainless steel. The office was overheated, and already decorated with a small Christmas tree, stars and streamers. Amanda snuffled behind the reception desk. The poor girl seemed to be sagging in all departments, starting with her liquid eyes. A combination of warm air and a cold virus, Evie imagined, plus, she had heard, trouble with the boyfriend, who probably did not fancy early invalidism.

"Hello." Amanda handed Evie her 'Thanks from a grateful family' Christmas letter and then disappeared in a burst of sneezing in search of a further supply of tissues. Evie opened the envelope. The card featured an inebriated Santa. The cheque was more generous than usual though, no doubt, tax deductible. As she slipped the contents into her handbag she saw the small silver box the doctor had given her. She was reluctant to open it. Should she wait for Christmas Day? The decision weighed her down. It must be the stifling atmosphere in the office. She walked to the window and tried to open that instead. Failure.

As she turned the box over in her hands, a fingernail caught the clip and the lid sprang back. Inside, on a miniature white satin cushion, were two scraps of newspaper. She unfolded them. One was the picture of the man who had shared part of her life, James

Dillaney; the other a paragraph describing how keen amateur footballer, Jim Dillaney, had died after apparently falling down the stairs at his home. She examined both cuttings closely as if they might speak to her. They were dated from the late 1970s. So much had happened at the time, suspicious policemen and unpleasant neighbours, that she had forgotten that her husband's death had made the local papers.

Evie sat down at the receptionist's desk. She wondered again what Dr Petters had meant by her secret. There was no such thing, she told herself out loud. It was an accident, but that didn't excise the image of a crumpled body.

Amanda reappeared, red nose temporarily staunched.

"Hello," she said, with what appeared to be the mainstay of her conversation. The girl glanced down at the desk and saw the newspaper cuttings spread out on the blotter pad. Before Evie could stop her Amanda had picked up the grainy reproduction and was studying it intently.

"That's my Dad," she screamed. "Where did this picture come from?" She looked at Evie as though she was accusing her of robbery. Tears began to choke out her cold.

"I know it's my Dad," she said, "even though I never saw him." Her voice was agitated. "Mum kept his photograph by her bedside. She said that he had died before I was born. When she died she made me promise to keep his picture."

It had started as an ordinary day, just before Christmas. Routine: work, home, supper, TV and bed. Now everything – or was it everybody? – was falling apart. Amanda was not, in Evie's experience, an overly emotional girl and the present display seemed genuine. Perhaps James Dillaney was trying his hand at reconciliation, in an odd way. It would be in keeping with the man; an early Christmas present for two of his women. Evie felt rather old to suddenly become an adoptive mother, and if she had taken the step voluntarily would she have chosen Amanda? Probably not. However, Christmas was approaching and she should be charitable, even if she regretted it later.

She paused and studied the girl. "You and I have something in common, Amanda." Amanda looked puzzled. "Get your coat and close reception," Evie added. "They should be capable of answering the telephone upstairs. I'm taking you for a glass of wine and a chat. That new bar in The High has had good reviews."

As the pair stepped out a black cat shot across their path. "That's good luck," Amanda said. Evie clutched at the little box that she had stuffed into her jacket pocket. She was not so sure.

Wallace Takes a Loo Roll to University
Yvonne Hands

We took Wallace to the station to help him carry his suitcases after the Christmas vacation. I left them to go to the Ladies, and when I came out and looked across the platform to the frosty northbound side and saw Wallace standing there surrounded by his suitcases ready to go off, I felt very sad. However, there were a lot of people I knew on the London side and I smiled warmly at the vicar and chatted to the Rector of Exeter College. And then to Betty Jeffries and Jean Newman, whom I absolutely can't stand. I gave a very cool nod indeed to Page-Connelly who was going off to Paris with his girlfriend, to show my disapproval. I feel we older dons' wives should set a standard to the younger dons.

When I got to the other side, I told Wallace what a sad thing it was to see your son off. I couldn't help but think of all those mothers in the First World War who had seen their sons off to Flanders from this very station. No one knew what mothers suffered. Wallace said he did. If there was one thing he knew, it was what mothers suffered. He apologised for not going off to Flanders Field to die. In any case, it wouldn't be any good going off to Flanders to die on this side. This side went to the North. If he'd been a soldier, he would be shot as a deserter for getting on the train on this platform, and going north. Just think how much I would have suffered as a mother if I'd sent my son off on the wrong platform to be shot as a deserter.

"Never mind," he said kindly. Perhaps there would be another war soon, and I could wind his puttees on and see him off, especially if I sent him in the opposite direction to the battle. He said Scotland must be full of old soldiers looking for Flanders.

On the subject of suffering mothers, he said he was wondering why I was walking round with a toilet roll on the end of a piece of string. Was it for him? What a lovely farewell gift. A yellow toilet roll. His favourite colour. But, he said, he had to point out that they did have toilet rolls in Lancaster. They had arrived in the North. Not too long ago, true, but they were there now.

Wallace said it would go with the three suitcases of dirty clothes he was taking back with him. It all fitted in. No! No! He didn't mind taking all his clothes back dirty to college and washing them there himself. What did it matter if everyone else was going back with suitcases full of clean, starched clothes? At least he had a clean toilet roll. He said he hoped the toilet roll WAS clean. It was just the same at half-term when everyone else had gone back with suitcases full of home-made cakes and home-baked bread. He'd gone back with a quarter of a loaf, which was mouldy when he looked at it, and a black banana. But he could see a background like this freed him from the humdrum; whilst his fellow students at university would end up doing boring jobs at merchant banks and filling in at Gstaad and the Bahamas, for him, the whole spectrum of society from the upper working class down to the homeless, was open.

"Dorothea," said Bassily. "Wallace is talking about the toilet roll on a piece of string that you have looped over your arm and dangling around your legs. Look," he said, "down there."

I looked down and saw it, a toilet roll hanging from a piece of string on my wrist. I looked at it a long time. Then I looked at Bassily. I remembered hanging my handbag on the door in the Ladies' lavatory, where there was a yellow toilet roll hanging on a piece of string. Then I looked across at the London platform and saw Page-Connelly and his girlfriend looking at me, and the vicar and the Rector of Exeter College. And that bitch Betty Jefferies. All looking at my toilet roll. I said to Bassily that I had to run away to sea and be a sailor. Now, this minute. Bassily said I was too old.

Just at that moment the northbound train came in and Wallace opened the door of a compartment. A military looking gentleman with a moustache asked Wallace to come in if he was coming. Yes, said Wallace, he was coming in for a long time. He was Captain Oates in reverse. He told the compartment at large that he would put his suitcase in the corridor so the smell wouldn't offend them. It was full of dirty clothes he was taking back to university. His mother, he said, pointing to me, had not had time to do them. The carriage looked at me and I explained that the dirty clothes were the result of a lack of communication. Wallace said they were the result of a lack of washing. Look, she'd brought him a toilet roll as a parting gift. He said he doubted if there was a chap in his college who'd been given such a useful present; it made a man stand tall. His mother was a fundamentalist, dealing with life at rock-bottom. The carriage looked at the toilet roll. Wallace pressed them to pass it round. Someone said it didn't look very new. No, said Wallace, that was the lovely thing about his mother, it was broken in first. It was a toilet roll that belonged to mankind. A toilet roll that had seen action, one could almost see the snow on its boots, as it were.

The porter started to close the door. Wallace did his Nazi salute to us, which he always does. He said to Bassily, "*Auf Wiedersehen, Adolf*," and to me, "*Auf Wiedersehen, Eva.*" Then he said, "*Gott mit uns*," which was on the caps of the SS. The gentleman with the large moustache got up and stumped into the window seat of the next carriage. Wallace got into his vacated seat, then he got up and hung out of the window and looked at the moustached gentleman in the next carriage. He pushed the yellow toilet roll on to his seat. He said it was his colour. It matched his eyeballs. Then he said we'd better go as he didn't like station farewells, even if he wasn't going to Flanders Field. Just then the stationmaster tapped the moustached gentleman on the shoulder and said he would like to have a word with him about removing station property.

Winter
Jenny Burrage

Days of bleakness and iced-up landscapes when
Sharp silvered stars stick points into the sky,
Pricking the still night far above our eyes,
Forcing us to listen to its cold cry.
The ripeness of autumn times now is lost,
Its leaves kicked under hedgerows by the wind
Trampled under sparklets of glittered frost.
Making bright red and gold memories dimmed,
Replaced by the passionless shape of trees
Crouching miserably on barren ground,
Like inky scarecrows against winter's freeze,
Unaware of white snowdrop clumps we've found.

Billy
Graham Bird

Billy had lived at the bottom of the heap ever since he was six, when his mother made him clean the shoes for his two older brothers before school. At thirty-two, Billy was used to it. He worked in the basement of a publishing company in Oxford, taking the post around the six-storey building every morning, then collecting the new letters and packages in the afternoons. All the girls in the building ignored him, every single one, and all the married ones too. He tried to be cheery, telling a few feeble jokes here and there, but always failed to make any lasting impression. Most people didn't know his name.

"Make sure that parcel gets to the courier before four o'clock," announced one particularly fiery dragon that Wednesday afternoon.

"Yes, Miss Prim," muttered Billy as he raced off with it under his arm before she could check what he'd said. He liked to give everyone names: there was Miss Prim, Miss Goat, Ms Cassidy – he called her that because she was so butch. The men were easy too: Mr Grumpy, Mr Big, Lord Posh.

Everyone has to be liked by somebody, and Billy had one admirer: Alice. Alice worked in the post room too, keeping the boxes clean and sorting the mail into floors ready for delivery. The trouble was that Billy didn't really like Alice that much. She was okay but he preferred Miss Leggy in accounts, now *that* was someone special. Alice was too much like him – scruffy, poor and plain.

"When will I ever find a man like you, Billy?" Alice said as he struggled through the door with Miss Prim's parcel.

"This one's for the Post Office, I'll take it down now. What do you mean, a man like me?"

"Oh you know, strong and handsome, someone to sweep me off my feet. Someone to take me to the Christmas party next week." Alice sat, polishing her nails and gazed over at him. He'd seen that gaze before.

"I need to rush, see you later." Billy hurried out, straight through reception and out onto Walton Street, the box balanced on his shoulder.

As he started to turn the corner into Beaumont Street, Billy stumbled, the box flew into the road and he fell in front of a large blue car. Billy was thrown up into the air and the force of the impact caused his shoe to fly off and all the way over to the other side. Billy landed with a crunch on the tarmac and passed out.

"Just try to keep still, Mr Preston." Billy opened his eyes and tried to focus on the smart nurse with a smiling face who was holding his leg. Billy thought he looked like a fairy godmother holding up a wand, except this was a man about to attach a splint. Next to the nurse stood a scruffy old witch, presumably the doctor, pressing on his toes till they hurt.

"Ouch, ouch what happened?"

"You were hit by a car. It seems you stepped out in front of it, but you're in safe hands now, Mr Preston."

"Call me Billy." He tried to smile.

Once they'd finished strapping his foot, the doctor and nurse left him alone in the cubicle and Billy lay back, contemplating his lot. What a day! What happened to the parcel? What about Miss Prim, would she have him fired? Had anyone missed him? What about going home? Would he miss the Christmas party? And Alice, she'd be worried.

The curtain was pulled back and in strode Tom and Terry, his two brothers.

"What have we here then, Billy? What have you been doing? Phone call said you might be a goner." Tom always got to the point quickly. "Why did I waste my time coming down here for this? You look fine."

"He's such a waster," said Terry, as he sat down on the only chair by the bed and jabbed his finger into Billy's foot.

"Ouch, ouch, ouch, ouch. Go away you two. Who called you?"

"Our names are in your wallet apparently, loser. It's because you don't have any proper friends."

"We brought some grapes," said Tom, as he pushed two of them into his own mouth.

"They say you can go home later." Terry laughed. "Even they won't have you overnight. Want you out by Christmas."

Billy sighed and lay back, thinking his two brothers were the ugliest pair you'd ever put together in the same room, and he was lucky to have the handsome genes.

The noise of a small scuffle outside the cubicle quietened Tom and Terry down. A woman's voice.

"I insist on seeing all the men, everyone who has been admitted this afternoon. It's very important I deliver it personally." The voice was young, upper class, like a princess, Billy thought.

"Well, please be patient Miss. I'll take you through each cubicle in turn," said the nurse.

"I'm Lady Belinda Carrington. You may call me Belinda."

"Yes, my Lady."

After a few minutes, the curtain was pulled back and Billy stared up to see the nurse and Lady Belinda. Tom and Terry just sat, entranced. They were all speechless.

Lady Belinda was tall, towering over the nurse beside her. She was young, younger than Billy, and stood elegantly and serenely at the end of the bed. She was dressed in a long, dark red cashmere coat and she was immaculately groomed, like a pedigree horse turned out for Ascot. Not that Billy had ever seen a pedigree horse close to, but this woman exuded class from every pore of her body. On top of that, she was utterly gorgeous. She smiled at each man in turn and each one froze, their mouths stuck open, their eyes glazed.

In her hand, Billy saw his shoe.

"Now," she said, " I have a shoe here that belongs to some poor man who was involved in an accident on Walton Street earlier today. I wish to find him."

Tom recovered first.

"I lost that shoe today, my Lady. I was walking near the top of Great Clarendon Street when it came off and was grabbed by a little brat who ran off with it."

"Hmmm, let's see then. Try it on," she said.

Tom struggled with it but, of course, it was too small.

Then Terry had a go. "I was on my bicycle on Walton Street today, Miss, when a dog chased me and pulled it off my foot."

Billy just lay back and waited, enchanted by the beautiful princess before him, while Terry struggled to make the shoe fit.

"It's no good," said Lady Belinda, "let's try the next cubicle."

The nurse came to the rescue. "There's poor Billy here, he came in today after an accident. You could try him, I suppose. I know it seems unlikely."

Billy smiled up at the Lady who smiled back at him, a moment of magic passing between them.

The nurse took the shoe and gently fitted it to Billy's bandaged foot, but it was no good, his foot was still swollen.

"Ah well, never mind," said Lady Belinda. " I was hoping to find the man who lost it, so I could nurse him in my Chelsea home and help him recover while he keeps me company. I'll have to try the next cubicle."

Billy passed out.

"Come on then Billy, talk to me."

Billy opened his eyes. "Where's Lady Belinda? Where are my brothers?"

Alice smiled down at him. "This is a hospital and I've come to see how you are, and look after you."

"But, there was, surely.... Oh, never mind." He sighed. "You have a wonderful smile, Alice. I'd never noticed it before. Thank you for coming."

Alice kissed Billy gently on the cheek, then sat back and munched on a grape. "Who left these, Billy? They are lovely."

Minis And Mirrors
Penny Macleod

Oscar watched the cars swinging round, suspended on the steel track that ran round the factory floor. Red Mini, yellow Mini, black Mini, purple Mini. He had applied for the job on Deianna's instructions.

"You go get your ass down to the Cowley Plant, Oscar. Your Dad can drive me and the girls round to the cleaning jobs, so you can go do man's work makin' cars an' earnin' us good money."

Oscar and Deianna had left their Caribbean island twenty-six years ago and she had started up her cleaning business, in and around Oxford.

"Man, there's enough dirt and grease in this damp, damp town to keep hundreds of cleaning businesses happy," she had remarked. "If you can see it through the fog and the rain, is what I'm sayin'."

Month by month they had acclimatised to this noisy, dirty place – not easy after leaving the sparkling sea of St Marten's and its brilliant sunshine. Deianna had several clients in the large Aga-fired houses of North Oxford. But she and Oscar lived in the 'other' Oxford – the world of the BMW Car Plant, and the infamous Blackbird Leys Estate.

Six months after they arrived, Oscar had gone to train as a mechanical and electrical engineer. He enjoyed the work and had picked up his knowledge on the job over the course of about five years. Now when a car came off the line and into a bay for tests, he could operate on autopilot. Plug the lead into the diagnostic socket (on the driver's side of the car); read the message off the dash: 'Intake camshaft sensor'; check if the camshaft sensor is plugged in. If it is, then the chances are it's wrongly positioned, so then reposition it, and if necessary, replace it. Simple.

Simple – but a highly responsible job. If a car involved in a serious accident was found to have a faulty camshaft sensor, it could be traced back to the engineer on the shift when the tests had been run. Everything was logged and recorded, car by car, serial number by serial number. If a fault was proven, then the engineer on duty could, in theory, be sued, not the company.

The days of Oscar's happy-go-lucky life on a Caribbean island were distant. With cold and damp came responsibility, and the Protestant work ethic.

Oscar had done well – he had been given a contract within a year and help with his mortgage as soon as he and Deianna were able to put down a deposit on their council house. And now he was one of the senior engineers, and liked to be a father figure to some of the younger men.

"Why you so respectful to the managers, Oscar?" Josh, the twenty-year-old trainee, said as he looked at Oscar through the windscreen. They were working together on a car that had come off the line into the testing bay.

"I like a quiet life."

"You take too much of their shit. Like that Codger – he's well out of order the way he treats you. Me and the lads expect a bit of trouble with him. But you been here twenty-five years, and he bullies you. You should grass him up to the Union."

"No, I don't wanna go there."

"Why not, man? We could have some major fun."

"We ain't here for fun, Josh. Plug the diagnostic lead in will you?"

"Yeah, yeah, Oscar. Why you so anal about this stuff, man?"

"Josh, these Minis are goin' all over the world. You want someone to die on a hairpin bend on a mountain road in Greece 'cos you didn't check the ABS system while it was on the Rollin' Road test?"

He looked hard at Josh.

"That don't matter, you'll pick up any mistakes I make."

"You gotta start takin' responsibility now, Josh. Time you was growin' up and thinking about givin' something back."

"Nah, then I'd be like you and have to deal with Codger. Watch out, Oscar! Here comes Codger with his Todger."

Oscar took Deianna along to the Long Service Awards ceremony organised by the German bosses of the company. It was conducted with genuine appreciation and a German sense of occasion. The Christmas tree in the large recreation room was decorated in the German style: white lights and handmade wooden angels, stars, and soldiers. *Kaffee und Kuchen* were served afterwards. A large German director with silver hair beamed at Deianna, who had her mouth full of cake.

"I think your husband has earned his cake today, *nicht wahr?*"

"Yeah but he's got a big enough belly already – you know what I'm sayin'?"

Oscar was presented with his medal commemorating twenty-five years of service by the large German director. He felt very proud of his achievement and placed it on the mantelpiece. Deianna did not officially congratulate him, but he caught her polishing it before her friends came round for their Friday night wine and gossip.

The next week Oscar was on the night shift. He picked up two cars without their intake camshaft sensor plugged in within an hour. Wandering over to the line, Oscar had a word with the guys on the production line. There was Josh, looking the worse for wear.

"Look Josh, you know it's three strikes and you're out."

"Don't be so heavy, man."

"I've broken the rules to come and warn you."

"Was you always, like, so stressed about stuff, Oscar?"

"No, things were easier twenty-five years ago. And I can remember guys then, they told me stories goin' back to the seventies and that. They'd come into work on the night shift in them days and take a nice kip. Standards were different then and the unions ruled."

Josh looked bored. "I don't like havin' to wear this uniform. It sucks."

"Me, I like that I don't have to think what I'm gonna wear in the morning."

"Yeah, you do man. You have to decide between your boilersuit and the trousers with jacket."

"Watch it, Josh."

"And it's well hard to choose out of the red, blue or yellow T-shirts."

"Josh, that's enough attitude from you, boy. Just keep awake and make sure the sensors are plugged in. I can only protect you so far. If there's another unplugged sensor in the next hour, I'll have no choice but to alert the Manager."

"Who's on duty?"

"Codger."

Josh groaned. "OK man, I know you're tryin' to help."

The next fault came up after twenty minutes. Oscar decided he was going to let it go; with any luck, Codger wouldn't notice. He would give that Josh a bollocking when Codger went for a rest break. Then Oscar looked up and saw Codger walking down the line. He was wagging his finger at Josh and a couple of other young lads. Then he strode towards Oscar.

"Well?"

"Yes, Mr Codger?"

"Isn't there something you should have reported to me?"

"I'm really sorry, Mr Codger – I just realised – there's been three strikes down the line…"

"And why have you 'only just realised'?" Codger's voice dripped sarcasm.

"I'm not on the ball tonight, sir. I think I might be going down with a virus or something."

"This is a serious omission. It raises disciplinary issues."

Ten minutes later Codger had gone on his break, and Josh went to look for Oscar. He darted in and out of the cars; a long line of two hundred of them, fresh off the assembly line, ran the length of the building. He found Oscar in the Test Suite area.

"Oscar, Oscar!" Josh shouted above the noise of the machinery that never stopped.

"Hello Josh." Oscar inserted the gauge between the door panel and the 'A' post at the side of the windscreen. It was two millimetres off.

"You shouldn'a done that."

"Done what?" Oscar loosened the nuts. "Here, hold this ratchet for me."

"Why did you cover up for me? You'd given me a warning, you didn't have to do that."

"I been talkin' to your mum." Oscar's hands were always cold in the winter, and he struggled with the torque bit, trying to loosen the screws on a door hinge. "She's told me about your dad losin' his job and how she needs you to help her with money for Christmas. You better hang on to this job, man, or your little brother and sister won't have no presents."

Josh stepped in with the ratchet, and with a deft twist, loosened the bolt on the bracket attaching the door to the car.

"And you're a natural mechanic, Josh. Don't get yourself sacked."

"You fancy my mum, Oscar. I seen you lookin' at her."

"Shut up, Josh and get back to the line before Codger sees you here."

The next day Oscar was called in to a meeting with Codger and the Union Representative. Codger announced that Oscar would be brought before a disciplinary hearing the following month. Furthermore, his attempt to shield the young man from trouble was likely to cost him his job. Outside, the Rep was not very hopeful.

"If it'd been like, a genuine mistake, mate, we wouldn't have had a problem. But he's on to you. Knows you've been watchin' out for that Josh."

"First time I've messed up in twenty-five years," said Oscar.

Deianna was furious. "You can't go losin' your job – we got a mortgage to pay. How did it happen, anyway?" She was even more furious when he told her what he'd done.

"You know what I'm sayin? I reckon you been behavin' different lately. You're clean out of your head, Oscar."

Oscar wondered why she always brought cleaning into it.

For the next two weeks Oscar kept his head down and worked even harder than usual. He was careful not to seek Josh out, and Josh, who had heard about Oscar's troubles, was now trying hard to be reliable. Codger sauntered by on his inspection round and smirked at Oscar. He was enjoying Oscar's agony.

"Such a shame you had to throw it all away after twenty-five years," he snarled, when no one else was nearby. "So difficult to get a new job at your age, what with the credit crunch an' all. Or, *mate*, you could always go back where you came from."

Oscar said nothing. Inside, he was seething. Down the line, he could see the silver-haired German director making a rare appearance. He was talking to Josh.

Oscar took his sandwiches at break and went to the Mirror Tent. The antique tent had been set up by the Creation Theatre Company in a corner of the BMW car park, and they performed plays there in the winter.

It was a sanctuary for Oscar where he could go and think. A couple of stage hands had been setting things up for the next day's performance, and they asked him to turn the lights out when he went. Oscar finished his sandwich, then turned out all the lights except for the red spotlight trained on the stage. He went and stood in the spotlight, eating a mince pie.

"All the world's a stage." He surprised himself with the sound of his own voice resonating round the tent. "And all the men and women merely players…" He coughed on a mince pie crumb. Then another voice came.

"They have their exits and their entrances. And one man in his time plays many parts." The voice spoke in a German accent. "I'm pleased to know that they taught you Shakespeare on your island, Oscar."

Another spotlight appeared, illuminating the German director sitting at the back of the tent.

"They taught us a bit, sir, but mostly I picked it up from the performances here in the tent."

"I understand. Takes you out of yourself?"

"Yes, sir."

"Makes you forget your troubles, of which you have a few right now?"

Oscar couldn't reply. He bit his lip.

"This time of year – it heightens everything, *nicht wahr*? I always think it's as though there's some force at work. You feel it when the lights sparkle in the darkness."

Chills ran down Oscar's spine. The fairy lights round the walls of the tent illuminated slowly, as though someone was operating a dimmer switch. The walls and ceiling of the tent were decorated with tiny mirrors which reflected the lights, and with sapphire, emerald and ruby-coloured stained glass drops. The glass drops danced as though a breeze had caught them. It occurred to Oscar that there was no breeze, though.

"I've cancelled the disciplinary committee for next month."

"Sir?"

The director pierced Oscar with his blue-eyed gaze. "And your record remains unblemished."

"I can't thank you enough, sir."

"No need. Josh is going to turn out as an excellent mechanic. Already he's working much better." The director winked at Oscar. Oscar smiled.

"His mother is a good-looking woman," said the director.

"How did you…?" Oscar trailed off.

"It happened to me once. Women can have that effect on us, *nicht wahr*?"

Words had deserted Oscar.

"It's powerful when it happens. I know. We'd better turn the lights out now – break is finished, yes? You will have some good news for your wife tonight."

The German director's eyes twinkled. Just like the mirrors reflecting the lights in the tent, thought Oscar.

Cinder
Jenny Burrage

Long red hair she had. She was wearing one of them handkerchief things over her boobs but you could still see them. Dead cool. Suddenly she walked over to me. She was better lookin' than all them Page 3 Babes.

"Hello you," she said in one of them posh voices, an' close up her eyes were as green as traffic lights. "I don't know you, do I? What's your name?"

"George," I said, "but everyone calls me Cinder on account of me being a cadet firefighter. Get it? Cinder – the shit at the bottom, that's me."

I looked up into those big green eyes and she laughed and laughed and her laugh sounded like them tinkling wind chimes what hung down in the old shop where I got tattooed.

"Come on Cinder," she said. "We've got an awful lot of catching up to do."

She took both my hands in hers and pressed her lips hard on mine and wedged her tongue inside my mouth. I could feel a stud underneath my tongue like a little marble.

"Happy Christmas, Cinder," she whispered in my ear.

She took me upstairs, stepping over the snoggers and smokers on the way up, to this gi-normous bedroom, all mirrors – even on the ceiling – and white, white everywhere. Our whole place in Blackbird Leys would of fitted inside that room. Awesome! There must 'ave been about ten bottles of champagne all lined up on a dressing table with some of them tall glasses next to them. She poured me one and then another, don't know 'ow many I drunk. Next minute she was taking off my clothes one by one ever so slowly. People kept coming in the room and I felt a right wuss. She didn't seem to care if people was watching. Then when I was starkers she slipped off her skirt an' she was naked underneath. She started pouring champagne all over me. We was soon lying on like this furry rug thing an' you can guess what 'appened next. To tell the truth I wish I could remember more about it but I was too far gone by then.

Now I know you're thinking, how did some poor young bloke like me get to meet up with a girl like 'er? Amazing, weren't it? Well my old mate Jules asked me if I'd like to go to a Christmas party in Norham Gardens, Saturday night. He fancies himself mixing with the Oxford toffs, does Jules.

"An' what would I effin' well wear?" I asked him.

"It's smart casual," he told me. I could of hit the bugger.

Anyway he lent me his old leather jacket and a spare pair of chinos. Mom bought me some new Nike trainers out of the family allowance and there I was, hair spiked up and ready.

"You look wonderful, George," she said.

"You look silly, George," shouted my little brother, Leyton.

I was just about to cuff him one when Mom told me Jules had arrived. I wish you could 'ave seen the motor he was driving. It was one of those old open-topped Morgan cars, worth a few grand.

"Where did you get it?"

"Don't ask," he muttered. "Just get in."

It was a mansion that place. There was a great big Christmas tree with all coloured lights in the front garden. The front door was open. Inside, people was like standing about with glasses or joints in their 'ands and all talking loudly like they were trying to drown each other out. Jules kept starin' at me.

"None of them clothes fit you," he said. "The trousers are too long and the jacket don't do up." I could of hit the bugger.

There wasn't no sign of any food but there was plenty of booze. Jules an' me stood there and then he moved off in the direction of a vodka bottle. It was then I saw her and she saw me. That girl. You know the rest.

Jules had to get the car back to wherever he'd got it from by the morning but I don't remember the ride back home. Mom said I crashed in the door, threw up on the carpet and went upstairs like a zombie.

Next time I saw Jules I asked him if he knew anything about the girl. He said her name was Cressida and there was no chance of me an' 'er ever getting it together.

"Out of your league, mate," he said.

I could of hit the bugger.

Ode to Joy?
Julie Adams

Dieter tutted as he approached the college doorway. The notice quite clearly stated that smokers must not stand within twenty feet of the entrance, yet there were several crushed cigarette butts within 40% of the permitted limit.

During his undergraduate years in his native Germany he had grown accustomed to the prevailing *laissez faire* culture, but Dieter had hoped when he won the bursary enabling him to do an MSc in Computing Science at Oxford, that the other students would be as serious-minded as he thought himself.

Dieter probably held the University's record for the student who had moved rooms most times during the first term. On the first staircase where he had a room his fellow students were too untidy, so he asked to move to a section with only girls. They were too noisy so Dieter asked to move to an area reserved for graduate students, but discovered that postgrads, having more experience, merely paced themselves better, partying harder and longer.

Dieter tried to tell his neighbours that they should close the shower door and put wrappings and tissues in the bin, but they ignored him. He placed a laminated notice on his door '*Ordnung muss sein!*' There must be order. Someone took a scalpel to it and carefully excised the U and an N, altering the notice to '*unOrdn g muss sein!*' The incorrect capitalisation offended Dieter as much as the vandalism, and the College Bursar made him pay for repairs to the scratched door, as he was the one who had first affixed an unauthorised notice. Eventually, after viewing alternative accommodation in several buildings, Dieter chose an ensuite room on a corridor for couples. They, in turn, soon complained about him because of the heavy-handedness of his nocturnal typing.

The college staff at first tolerated Dieter's eccentricities, realising that at least they weren't cultivated, like the tweed-wearing pipe smokers or the morose Goths who could be seen laughing at reruns of the 'Vicar of Dibley' in the JCR. It was generally expected that students would have relinquished their more annoying affectations by the time they reached postgraduate status, but Dieter's lack of self-awareness made him oblivious to the effect he had on those around him. Now every time he entered the bursary all eyes were on him, which Dieter interpreted as professional attentiveness to his latest litany.

Like many who expected others to stick rigidly to the prescribed rules, Dieter himself felt that he could ignore those that did not suit him. He was refused entrance to Hall for the first special dinner during Michaelmas term as he failed to wear a gown. The Chief Steward had some experience in dealing with those students who thought they could accept all of Oxford's academic advantages while rejecting its customs and traditions, and politely but firmly refused to admit Dieter to the dining hall. Dieter tried to argue his way to his dinner:

"But in Germany we never wear these costumes." The Chief Steward clearly saw this information as irrelevant to the daily life of an Oxford college, and Dieter compounded his error by adding, "Except perhaps in Heidelberg University, which is the oldest university in the world."

The next day the Dean informed Dieter that he could wear the gown as required, or forfeit a term's worth of prepaid dinners in Hall. Dieter's financial prudence won out and he slunk off to The Campus Stores in The Broad for his scholar's gown and mortar board.

Once admitted to the dining hall for meals, Dieter earned the hostility of the serving staff and hungry fellow students by asking for the food to be placed on his plate in a particular order and in specific places, holding up the servery queue as he went to and fro along the hot food counter. He failed to understand that making an unreasonable request politely does not render it acceptable.

Shortly after his interview with the Dean Dieter missed his first Matriculation ceremony by again attempting to enter without the required academic dress. The University Proctors were less patient with him than the college's Chief Steward had been. When it became clear that no amount of reasoning or petulance would gain him admittance to the Sheldonian, Dieter hurried back to his room to change into *sub fusc*, but the University's Ceremonial Organist had finished the introit and the Latin ceremony had already started by the time he made it back.

There were several aspects of Dieter's behaviour that no one was ever able to explain; every time he changed accommodation the scouts immediately noticed an astonishing upswing in the amount of toilet paper being consumed, which returned rapidly to normal as soon as he moved to his next room. When Dieter moved into an ensuite room the housekeeping staff were finally able to pinpoint the tissue squanderer. They surreptitiously searched his room for the purloined toilet rolls, but found only the unusually large number of cardboard inner-tubes, arranged with precision on their ends in his recycling bin.

Dieter's studies progressed as unsmoothly as his domestic arrangements. His Tutor was accustomed to the particular vagueness of computing science students, whose brains often seemed to function only in binary code, but working with Dieter required a whole new approach. He soon forbade Dieter to begin any sentence with the words 'But in Germany…' and repeatedly explained that his submission for the weekly tutorial was not optional. Every time Dieter's (perfectly truthful) excuse was the same:

"I have nearly finished it but I need to look at it again…"

The Tutor admired attention to detail, but Dieter's perfectionism prevented him ever completing a piece of work and his unwillingness to show drafts meant that he could not benefit from early feedback.

"As I have told you repeatedly, any piece of hardware or software is only as good as its user interface. *Your* user interface is severely faulty; I cannot mark work that is invisible."

The Tutor, along with many others whom Dieter encountered in England, was unable to pronounce his name, usually plumping for 'Diet- er'.

"One pronounces it Dee-tare; I am not on a diet," he said, in a rare attempt at a joke. The Tutor (with almost unprecedented but wholly intentional provocation) eventually settled for 'Die-tare'.

"I want three practical pieces by the end of term, Die-tare. Just small projects, each written in a different programming language."

As long as he wasn't in front of them in a refectory queue, Dieter was popular with other students. His fellow Germans were initially embarrassed by him, fearing that the UK in general would form the impression that his behaviour was somehow typically Teutonic. However, it was readily apparent that Dieter would have been beyond '*ordentlich*' in any culture. Once he was able to arrange his accommodation according to his own liking in an ensuite room, Dieter's energy, enthusiasm and organisational skills were put to good use in several student societies, rather than being inflicted on his neighbours.

Dieter settled into his self-imposed routine for the rest of October and the first two weeks of November, managing to alienate further members of staff, including the subject librarians from both the Computing Science and Engineering departments. They chased him constantly for books he had borrowed in Noughth week and would not return despite urgent requests from other students. The librarians (and his fellow students) would have been even more furious had they known that the books were sitting neatly ordered on Dieter's shelves in Dewey Decimal ranks, unopened, and would not be returned until the day of his eventual departure from Oxford.

He was called in for a formative interview with the Dean again:

"I've been informed that you didn't matriculate in October. As you are on a one-year course you need to matriculate before Christmas so you can take your first exams in January."

"But in ..."

"No Matriculation, no exams, no degree," said the Dean, giving Dieter the date and time of the next ceremony.

Dieter's equilibrium was further shaken when, in mid-November, he entered the college one day to find a large Christmas tree outside the porters' lodge. He had noticed the proliferation of Christmas decorations already in the shops on arriving in Oxford in early October. This felt inappropriately early to his German sensibilities, but to erect a tree in mid-November? Dieter commented to a passing student whom he knew from the film club,

"It's not normal."

The other student, a Brit, looked at the seven-foot tall spruce fir, covered in sparkling baubles, gaudy tinsel and multicoloured lights and said,

"Looks like a perfectly normal Christmas tree to me."

One evening, looking at a notice for the college's forthcoming carol service on 28th November, Dieter asked the Chief Steward why Oxford celebrated Christmas a month earlier than the rest of the world. The Chief Steward wondered, not for the first time, at the way in which the brightness of the intellect of many of these young people outshone the steady flame of common sense.

"We have to celebrate Christmas early because Michaelmas term ends in November."

"But in Germany…" Dieter started to say, looking at the tall, richly-decorated tree in front of one end of the dais, slightly obscuring the less illustrious end of High Table.

Dieter thought about the Christmas traditions at home in Germany. As soon as darkness fell on Christmas Eve, every family in the village would suddenly decide to take their children for a walk – whatever the weather – while one parent or grandparent stayed at home. On their return, the children would find that the Christ Child had visited, bringing with Him presents and a decorated tree. A *tastefully* decorated tree: invariably a real fir, with carved wooden figures from the Erz Mountains and real white candles (or often an electric version nowadays). After the distribution of presents Dieter's family would join in with carols broadcast from the octagonal church in Seiffen, a small hand-carved version of which sat on his mother's china cabinet.

The British display of seasonal vulgarity was repeated in the entrance of every university building Dieter visited over the next few days, but the worst awaited him in the entrance of the Computing Laboratory – an artificial tree with lights that flashed in a random sequence. He wondered at the gaudy tree's provenance and how many different parts of the Far East had contributed to its manufacture: the plastic-looking tree, the gimcrack baubles, the tinsel and lametta. He speculated further about the techie who had prostituted his programming talents to create the algorithm that made the lights flash in a random order. Algorithm. *A precise step-by-step plan for a computational procedure that begins with an input value and yields an output value in a finite number of steps.* An idea started to form in Dieter's mind, a precise step-by-step plan for a computational procedure that would satisfy his tutor's demands.

Over the next two weeks Dieter worked on his practical project. He couldn't educate the British in better Christmas taste, but he could do something about the flashing lights he saw most often. He visited the workshops of Engineering, the Computing Lab and Information Engineering, helping himself to a transputer or two, a movement sensor and some Field Programmable Gate Arrays. At night he wrote code, trying his hardest to type softly on his laptop keyboard, but by this time all of his neighbours were feverishly completing term assignments so wouldn't have heard him above their own typing noise.

He started with the tree at the busy entrance of the college. Dieter found some New Age pseudo-technology on a website selling an eye mask with lights in it claiming that certain frequencies of pulsed light induced a feeling of calm. He created a neat piece of code in Pascal programming language which described an inverse relationship between the flow of traffic past the movement sensor and the rapidity of the lights; when the college's entrance was empty, the Christmas lights would flash merrily, but at busy periods their flashing would slow to the soothing patterns described in the eye mask's advert.

Dieter waited until the early hours of the morning when the lobby was empty, and set to work attaching his piece of hardware to the junction box of the Christmas lights, mildly annoyed by the differences in British electrics: "Why are they so paranoid about earthing every single plug? It's not normal."

Next came the tree in the Computing Lab. He used a transputer and Occam programming language to reconfigure the flashing sequence so the different coloured lights represented dots and dashes to convey a variety of messages in Morse code:

"Fröhliche Weihnachten; gesegnete Festtage; einen guten Rutsch ins Neue Jahr." Merry Christmas, Season's Greetings, a good start to the New Year. He was sure that, as he had done, many of his fellow comp science students would have read 'Cryptonomicon' as teenagers, deciding to learn Morse code afterwards.

Finally, Dieter tackled the college's Hall. He gained entrance to the locked dining hall by telling one of the porters the truth:

"The Christmas tree is not decorated properly and I want to fix it." The porter seemed to find this explanation entirely in keeping with his expectations of Dieter's behaviour and unlocked the back door for him.

Dieter had previously searched the internet for the original source code for the 'Space Invaders' game and used it with Handel-C programming language and a Field Programmable Gate Array, instantly turning software into hardware. He wired the FPGA unit into the control box of the Christmas lights, and while the Fellows and their guests dined at High Table, an intergalactic battle was waged on the side of the tree facing the assembled students. Near the top of the tree blocks of red and green lights representing the aliens pulsed from left to right, moved down a row then moved from right to left. At the bottom of the tree a defender dodged from behind baubles to fire vertical streams of white lights at the invading aliens, smashing them to blue and yellow smithereens when they were hit. Given a joystick and a few more hours, Dieter could have made it all interactive.

Just hours before the submission deadline Dieter snapped a few digital photos of the trees and pasted them into his project along with the code and details of the hardware. The tutor would later describe several aspects of these applications as "roughly equivalent in sophistication to a baked bean tin and a wet piece of string", but was nevertheless pleased with the precision of the programming, the elegance of the code and the finish of the hardware. He admired Dieter's quirky imagination and guessed he might go far in the industry, particularly if he could improve his 'user interface' for dealing with people.

Dieter hurried back to his room, tidied it carefully, changed hastily into *sub fusc*, and walked briskly down The Broad to the Sheldonian just in time to enjoy the organ music and the camaraderie of Matriculation, his seasonal civilising mission accomplished.

Christmas Day
Birte Milne

This turned out to be one of the better ones.

But all the same, I spent a good half hour looking out on the bare trees along the Banbury Road before I could face getting out of bed. I honestly didn't know if I could get through another Christmas Day in this place. Then, I suppose there's every likelihood that this will be my last. This is my 88th Christmas. Quite a count. Quite a feat if I may say so myself, considering they all thought it was a matter of days when my hip went back in '91. Eighteen years on and I still keep them waiting and worrying about where my money is going.

To tell you the truth, I swear that's what keeps me going. Spending as much of their inheritance as I can before I call it a day. That and outliving Mrs Bagnol-Hocking, the old battleaxe.

Yes, yes, I know she's five years younger than me, but I can still beat her at Scrabble and I still have one good hip left to have a swing round on the floor in front of her with the handsome Mr Harrison. I smile sweetly when we pass her wheelchair leaving her to watch in envy with her one good eye. Do I feel guilty? You must be joking! Had enough years of thinking about what everybody else thinks. Now I couldn't care less. What's left of this life is for me to enjoy.

I know I did say I couldn't cope with another Christmas, but to be truthful this one was much better than the other ones I've had here at The Court. Lucinda, of course was in her usual bossy mode, thinking she was in charge of the proceedings. She gave me one of her 'if looks could kill' stares, when I ignored her table plan and manoeuvred myself in between her and sweet little Mr Fenton. He's such a darling. I'd let him pull my cracker any day. And I did, just as Lucinda was about to make her usual boring speech. I don't need that Lucinda to tell me when or with whom I pull my cracker. I think she got that message loud and clear when I told her to 'put a sock in it'. Made all the others giggle and pull theirs too, just to prove a point. She softened up a bit when she'd had a few sips of her Asti Spumanti and Mr Fenton took pity and pulled her cracker too.

Our Christmas dinner was the best present we could have wished for. Our usual useless cook was away and we had the most delicious food cooked by one of the volunteers and her gorgeous boyfriend. Not the usual mashed-up vegetables and synthetic-looking meat which just make you wish you could be tube fed instead. The turkey! Oh, the juiciest you could imagine and stuffed with apricot and cranberries. Potatoes roasted to perfection for even the most troublesome dentures. Vegetables tender and firm, just as I used to do them myself and the *gravy*... Not even Albert losing his top dentures into his sparkling Asti, nor Pandora's usual lack of bladder control coinciding with the serving of seconds, could put any of us off blissfully savouring every delightful mouthful of this amazing meal.

An air of peace descended over us all after the meal as we sat dreaming of Christmases past. Lucinda showed her human side by offering to share the precious box of After Eights she'd had from her son for Christmas. We managed to be civil to each other long enough to sing a few carols without anyone complaining, and after that even agree on which channel the TV should be on. For once it just didn't seem worth kicking up a fuss at having to watch 'Only Fools and Horses' for the umpteenth time.

I've hidden the last cracker. I'll ask Mr Harrison if he wants to pull it later. I'm hoping for just one more Christmas miracle.

The Christmas Cake – A True Story
Robin Courage

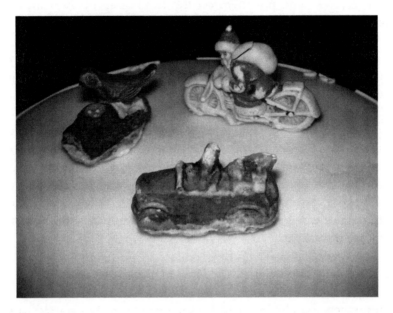

Each child held a candle, some with older ones helping. Robin's eight grandchildren had been wide-eyed with wonder during the afternoon children's service in Christ Church Cathedral, Oxford, on Christmas Eve 2008. They were used to their tiny church in the hills of Northumberland and found the grandeur of Christ Church awe-inspiring. Arriving back at their grandfather's home in Headington, the excitement of Christmas soon gripped them as they looked around the house, holly behind the pictures and, of course, the tree festooned with old and newer baubles.

Abigail, aged seven, noticed the decorations upon the Christmas cake on the sideboard.

"Grandad, why is Father Christmas sitting on a funny old motorbike, and he's got an ancient car too?"

"Those decorations belonged to my father and mother, your great-grandparents."

"Can I play with them?" asked Leila, aged four, on tiptoes,

trying to see.

"No, darling. They're very old now, as old as me. I bring them out every year and put them on the fresh icing of the Christmas cake."

"Why?" asked the three-year-old, Toby.

"They remind me of Ann and Guy. Many years ago, they would have also gone to the service at Christ Church, where we have just been."

"Why?" asked Toby.

"Well, these decorations have had a long and very special journey. My mother baked a Christmas cake for my father soon after I was born and put these very same decorations on the icing."

"What's so special about that?" asked ten-year-old Georgie.

"What is special, my darlings, is that my father was abroad, fighting in the Second World War when my mother, Ann, sent him the Christmas cake.

Robin's oldest child, Archie, said,

"Dad, why don't you tell the little ones the story after tea?"

Later, when the children had finished eating, Robin started to tell the story.

"My mother sent the Christmas cake decorated with Father Christmas on his motorbike and in his car to my father in time for Christmas 1944. I would have been four months old and my mother would not even have known in which country he was fighting Hitler's army."

Robin paused, reflecting on the endless wars that had desecrated the world ever since and picked up a book entitled 'The history of 15/19 The King's Royal Hussars 1939-1945.'

"You can read some of the story later in this book."

In the hot summer of 1939, Guy graduated with a degree in PPE from Christ Church College and joined the family regiment abroad. He returned safely from Dunkirk and later, whilst training at the Lulworth Tank Ranges, met Ann, a local girl, at a Lulworth officers' mess party.

While the British and American forces waited to invade the Continent, the Regiment had been training around Thetford Forest in Norfolk. Later Ann was to read in the book,

In the first week of August ('44) we collected a medley of Cromwells, Centaurs, and Shermans [tanks] and we started training once again on the Stanford Battle Area. We were allowed to take advantage of the slight lull to send all officers and men on two days' leave; most of the Regiment had had no leave for four to six months and this was a welcome respite after our hard work. We knew it must be the last chance.

On 6th August, Guy took the opportunity to meet his baby Robin who had been born four days earlier in a Dorset rectory, haunted by a friendly ghost. The Regiment received the command on 12th August 1944 to go to Havant the next day for embarkation to France. Ann was to read in the book,

No words can convey the excitement and rush of these last few hours. What would be in store for us? We did not even know what formation we were to join in France, or what role we should play. We had waited for years for this moment and now it had come.

Major Guy Courage D.S.O. July 1945, on the road to Kiel

Ann was still living with her parents in the rectory at Melbury Osmond, a hamlet in deepest Dorset. While Ann mixed a Christmas cake for Guy, she was thinking of the last time she had seen him, for two whole days at the beginning of August after giving birth to their son, Robin. There was that awful hollow feeling when they parted as she knew he would be soon going abroad to fight. Would he come back? His younger brother had already been killed.

She rode her bike, 'Algy', the five miles to Yeovil to buy some decorations to put on her freshly iced cake. They included a Father Christmas on a motorbike and another in an open top car; also a child sledging with arms outstretched. Although she planned to send the cake in September 1944 from Dorset, there was no way of knowing what chance there would be of its surviving war conditions. Of course, Guy's letters were censored and, frustratingly, his writing was so appalling she could only ever read part of it. She had been able to decipher just three words of his first letter!

She hoped that by sending the cake early, there was a possibility of it reaching him in time for Christmas, despite his squadron being constantly on the move in Europe.

Ann did not dare think whether he would even still be alive. She would not know until later when she read the history of the Regiment in the war, that by then he was around Etrepagny in Belgium pursuing the battered German army.

No description can do justice to the discomfort and weariness of it all – perpetual drenching rain, frequent halts, feverish consultation with others to find the correct route, hurried reference to the map, and, above all, the constant struggle against sleep.

Ann left her two-month-old baby boy with her mother in Melbury and mounted 'Algy' to deliver her parcel containing the Christmas cake, complete with the new decorations, to the Lulworth Ranges Officers' Mess. The orderly showed unfounded confidence in its delivery. The cake would take a tortuous route from Dorset, to an as yet unknown destination, via the supply echelons.

The next day, the package joined other mail on a stores' lorry containing spare parts for tanks and other fighting vehicles, bound for Poole Harbour. A crane hoisted the stores in cargo nets on board a steamer which went across the Channel in convoy. The boat arrived at the Mulberry Harbour in Arromanches which was now properly signed and organised with military police controlling traffic, very different to the chaos when Guy had arrived there on 15th August 1944. Then eighty per cent of his Regiment had succumbed to seasickness as there had been a violent storm during their night crossing from Portsmouth. At least their landing in France had been peaceful, without meeting the German defence which others less fortunate had encountered on D-Day.

The supply echelons had trouble keeping up with the rapid advance of the British army across France. The aim was to refuel tanks under cover of darkness, but this was not always achieved and sometimes there was barely time to transfer all the goods, leaving less important items like mail to catch up another day. Also, it had been raining heavily all autumn from early September, making the rough roads heavy going for the lorries.

The route took the convoy over the temporary Bailey bridge across the river Seine where Guy's tanks had crossed on rafts on 27th August 1944 before that bridge had been built. On that occasion, the problem had been how to reach the hilltop near Giverney, which was under enemy observation. Guy had laid a smoke screen while his tanks slowly ground up the escarpment in bottom gear. The next day, the Squadron had been sent to rout out some Germans from slit trenches in a cornfield. The trenches were covered by stooks of corn and an officer and two troopers had been killed while they rounded up prisoners. They had not realised some of the enemy were still hiding in the corn.

Now there were no such hazards and a better route had been found for the supply lorries, with friendly French waving as the convoy progressed north-east. The mail, including the decorated cake, was transferred to another lorry when the first became bogged down after sliding off the track in the heavy storms.

Ann received a letter from Guy 'somewhere on The Continent', which she later discovered was posted on 7th September 1944 near Antwerp, during a two-day break for maintenance, baths and letter writing. While the convoy travelled through Belgium, liberated crowds egged them on their way by waving and showering presents on the men. In this letter, Guy described how the Belgian children would cry:

> *'Cigarettes pour Papa.' Small children as young as six would then retire a short way, lighting up with pride and no thought for 'Papa'!*

Ann was the daughter of a vicar so she was put under pressure to have baby Robin baptised even though his father was away fighting. The Christening was planned for 28th October 1944. Guy's elder brother, Nigel, had been a prisoner of war in Germany since Dunkirk and fortuitously turned up unannounced the day before, minus a leg. Robin's godfather, Roy Swanwick, was home on leave and came to the ceremony.

The lorry, whose load included the cake, was commandeered for more important cargo as a result of another vehicle breaking down. The cake parcel, other mail, clothes, sleeping bags and so on replacing items lost whilst fighting, were placed in a farm building whose roof had been shot away at one end. A tarpaulin covered the pile.

> ...owing to the speed of the advance, they were passing through country which had not always been cleared of enemy infantry; this meant a lot of sentries and patrols for the drivers and other men travelling on the lorries.

A couple of days later, soldiers lifted the tarpaulin to reload the heap of stores back onto the lorry bound for the Regiment. They were startled to find two German infantrymen coming out with their hands up. The POWs were passed back down the line and the lorry finally rejoined the supply echelon, which was shortly to pass through the small village of Montgaroult. It was near this village that:

> C Squadron (Major G. Courage) shot up some enemy infantry and horse-drawn vehicles loaded with ammunition. Two of these turned out to be loaded with wine which had been looted by the Germans: unfortunately before advantage could be taken of this booty, C Squadron was ordered to draw back!

Some of this wine was now added to the lorry headed for the Regiment.

The supply echelon made steady progress to catch up with the Regiment, which a few weeks earlier had to cope with:

> ...*incessant rain, mud, congestion and bogged tanks; a sorry tale. The country was impassable and what tracks there were, were deceptive and liable to let a tank sink without warning.*

That had been the situation for much of November and had only marginally improved by the time the lorry carrying the cake and Father Christmas in his car, had caught up with the echelon.

By December 1944, the Regiment was in reserve in a sector of the Maas from Maeseyck to Roermond in Holland. Guy's squadron was in a farm in the hamlet of Baexem and they spent two months there, undertaking maintenance and training before progressing into Germany. This occupation was a considerable improvement on the previous two weeks:

> ...*the main feature was road making. The weather was generally wet and the roads became nearly impassable in a few days. They were only sandy tracks and appeared to be bottomless. Squadrons put loads of rubble from some bombed houses nearby into the local roads, but lorries continued to get stuck whenever they had to go out. We were fighting a losing battle with the roads and road making was voted an unpleasant task by all.*

Fog and rain continued to wreak havoc during December. Preparation for Christmas worked around the Squadron's operational commitment of being '*at readiness*' every third day:

> *We found the country behind the river Maas to be quite hilly and more interesting than most of Holland that we had seen so far.*

However, there was an impending crisis as the lorries containing the Christmas supplies had failed to arrive on time due to the dreadfully waterlogged roads. So a tracked recovery vehicle was dispatched with an armed escort to collect the lorry from the stranded supply echelon. However, when the lorry was towed back to the Regiment, the Quartermaster found it contained three tons of 'Compo' rations and ammunition for the tank guns, understandably deemed more important by the dispatching officer. The recovery vehicle and escort turned around with fresh crew, finally hauling the correct lorry into Regimental HQ just in time, two days before Christmas. Ironically, the next night there was a hard frost making the roads passable once again.

On Christmas Day 1944 the men shared gifts received from their families and the local Dutch population, in addition to the usual rations. Guy received the parcel which he opened with his best friend, Roy Swanwick. They both laughed when they saw Father Christmas in his car. Father Christmas was also on a motorbike which was just like the Regimental dispatch rider's.

> *Christmas Day again provided large dinners and much festivity, preceded by church services as always. Our Christmas was not unduly disturbed by the theory that the Boche was going to celebrate Christmas two days early and then put in a large-scale counter-attack on Christmas Day! Fortunately this was only a rumour.*

Guy was very taken by his young wife's efforts in having the beautifully decorated cake delivered. Though living in the country, she would still have had to scrounge to find the ingredients. How he longed to see her for real. Her photograph in his battle dress was so crumpled. He carefully wrapped the decorations, including Father Christmas on his bike and in his car, in clean gun-cotton waste and placed them in an old oil-filter box in the bottom of his rucksack.

*

"Here we are, children, 64 years later on Christmas Day again. The baby Robin was, of course, me. It is remarkable that my father survived combat to bring back the decorations and that my mother's Christmas cake reached him on the front line of battle. After all, once when his squadron's tanks were hiding in a wood, they were shot at by our own, friendly Spitfires, fortunately without casualties."

Robin looked pensive. "As you know his great friend, my Godfather, Roy Swanwick, attended my Christening but within four months he had been killed in his tank, just two months before the end of the war in Europe. My father saw Roy's tank *'brew up'* which must have been terrible for him."

The grandchildren followed Robin's eyes. "Look at the silver frame by the cake on the sideboard. The soldier in that photograph is Roy. My father wrote this history of the Regiment at war.

"As you see," Robin continued, "I still use these old Christmas decorations on my cake in Oxford each year and hopefully they will survive so that you can continue using them for many more years."

"Don't be sad, Grandad," said Abi, putting her arms round Robin's shoulders.

Georgie picked up the silver match box. "Let's light the candles."

"Grandad," asked little Toby, "how does Father Christmas get his car down the chimney?"

Notes

Getting Away for Christmas by Graham Bird

This story is a fictionalised account of a real accident which occurred just north of Oxford on Christmas Eve in 1874 in freezing snowy conditions. A broken metal tyre and poor braking procedures caused a derailment leading to the deaths of thirty-four people. This was the worst disaster on the Great Western Railway up to that time. An unnamed hero held up a wooden beam for an hour before firemen could rescue a trapped victim, providing inspiration for this story. More details of the incident can be found on the internet:

http://en.wikipedia.org/wiki/Shipton-on-Cherwell_train_crash or in an excellent non-fiction book by Peter R Lewis and Alistair Nisbet named 'Wheels to Disaster!: The Oxford Train Wreck of Christmas Eve 1874', published by The History Press, 2008.

Winter in Oxford by Yvonne Hands

The author, who travelled extensively in the Soviet Union, has on this occasion exercised artistic licence to relocate the KGB headquarters from the Lubyanka to the more picturesque Red Square, and to allow the KGB to continue to exist beyond 1991 without changing its name.

Christmas Presence by Dion Vicars

The Aztec crystal skull which inspired this story is actually held in the British Museum and can be safely viewed at:
http://tinyurl.com/nqtz8z

The Annunciation by Julie Adams

The fertility patient is actually singing part of the 'Magnificat' which features in many vocal pieces.

The Christmas Cake – A True Story by Robin Courage

This story is a slightly fictionalised account of the true story of the author's parents. The cake decorations survived their wartime journey and are still carefully brought out each Christmas. The quotes are taken from the 'The History of 15/19 The King's Royal Hussars 1939-1945' by Major G Courage DSO (the author's father), published in 1949 by Gale & Polden Limited, Aldershot.

The Authors

Since leaving Denmark in 1981 **Birte Milne** has seen it all: a Buddhist Lama cutting the lawn in flowing robes which match his orange Flymo, a white witch carefully scraping soot off the sitting room fireplace to use in her spells, and a Tibetan doctor creating a Buddhist retreat in her garden shed. Her writing draws on her experiences and the people she has been lucky enough to come across. She has had several plays performed and short stories published, and being a great optimist, she still believes she is going to finish *that novel* one day.

Dion Vicars was unable to spell or write at school and wisely moved into maths and computing, where he honed his skills producing documentation and reports. As a teacher he progressed to course notes and a few academic papers, but has since found that making it up is more fun. All this is an excellent background for the fabrication of pseudo-science. He is curious and amused by the way social systems and technology affect lives.

Graham Bird started writing fiction in 2004, and has published a number of short stories. He enjoys mystery characters with underlying tensions in their lives that reveal themselves slowly. He has recently researched stories set across different time periods and is working on a novel spanning generations.

Jenny Burrage is famous in her family for being able to read the newspaper at the age of four. She has been reading and writing ever since. At the moment she is working on a book about meerkats for the under-fives.

Julie Adams spent the first four years of her life in Germany and has loved the German language and people ever since. Nowadays she is more likely to hang out with computer scientists, and consequently can recognise a Field Programmable Gate Array at twenty paces. For several years Julie ran a postgraduate course but more recently wrote educational materials for OUP. She is currently working on a series of science fiction for teenagers. Julie lives in North Oxford, mostly in a dazed state induced by fertility drugs.

In a previous incarnation **Neil Hancox** wrote many technical reports and papers and co-authored two books on composite materials. Fascinating as this was he decided, on retiring, to try fiction. He enjoys writing surreal and often ambivalent stories which straddle the borderline between reality and fantasy. The characters usually start by doing what they are told, but often take over the story and do what they want. He hopes that none of them ever escape and press the key which deletes the author.

Out of all the jobs **Penny Macleod** has had, the one she enjoyed most was interviewing people for TV and Radio in Saudi Arabia. And now when she looks at people, she frequently asks *why?* and *what if?* Those questions bring ideas for stories, plays and screenplays. Penny also records material for Radio Cherwell and Listening Books, and dances salsa to keep sane. She is currently working on a screenplay about older women and younger men.

Robin Courage's travels through life have taken him from the Army and Management Consultancy to delivering yachts round Europe. Writing helps him to sit still occasionally. His grandchildren's fascination with a well-travelled heirloom Christmas decoration led him to write the story in this book. He enjoys writing poetry, and performed several of his poems at the 2007 Oxford Fringe Literary Festival.

When she retired **Val Watkins** thought it would be a great idea to try writing stories. After all, she had asked children to write stories during her teaching career, and brilliant they were, too. However when she did start writing she found that it was much harder than it looked. She has published several short stories. Val also likes writing plays suitable for radio, especially short plays with funny punch lines.

Yvonne Hands has been happily married to an Oxford don for many, many years, providing material for her ongoing project, which is a comic take on life as a North Oxford housewife. She loves spy stories and always felt her husband would have made a great spy; but as he was Oxford and heterosexual, she knew he didn't stand a chance.

Also available by the Turl Street Writers:

Turl Street Tales, published by arima Publishing.
ISBN: 978 1 84549 349 3

Our website: www.turlstreetwriters.com
Contact us: turlstreetwriters@gmail.com

Lightning Source UK Ltd.
Milton Keynes UK
14 August 2010
158401UK00002B/1/P